the New Marketing Basics

Basics

BECAUSE BASIC MARKETING
HAS CHANGED !

Thomas R. Leonard Jr.

and Bill Davis

ISBN-10:1463743890
ISBN-13: 978-1463743895

DEDICATION

To all of the Entrepreneurs everywhere who really are the people who make the world of business turn. Hoping that we can be influential in helping Entrepreneurs with direction in which they can start their Education. That can help determine his / her future in business.

A quote from William Cook "We are here, charged with the task of completing (one might say creating) ourselves."

This book can help us find the direction of our business and be able to take advantage of the latest and greatest tools and methods.

Let us thank our Publisher Createspace for all of their support.

Let's Go!

CONTENTS

Introduction   vi

Acknowledgements   viii

Disclaimer   x

1   the New Basics of Marketing   1

2   Time to Start Your Business Plan   6

3   Begin with a Message Your Pitch   11

4   Marketing Plan   18

5   a Winning Strategy   21

6   Branding   24

7   Marketing Methods and Techniques   29

8   Social Marketing / Media / Networking   63

9   Mobile Marketing   83

10   Targeting Your Marketing Efforts   98

11   Polishing Your Marketing   108

Glossary   121

About the Authors   127

Introduction

NMB What is marketing? Most people have an idea what marketing is. It's trying to sell something to someone, right?

Well, that's basically right, but there's a lot more to it than that. Marketing is the methodology that you use to get your product into a consumer's hands.

It used to be in the old days that you would advertise in the Yellow Pages, you could run weekend ads in the newspaper and if you wanted to go big, you would run your ad in a local magazine. You would consider direct mail, or you might even have a weekly event.

There are a lot of different things that you did 10 or 20 years ago, and now you have so many more methods of marketing.

Where do you start?

Wow, things have really changed in marketing. You now have twitter, Facebook, Digg, MySpace, LinkedIn, and on top of all this you would have your own blog or maybe even a website.

That's for starters. Now you need to start looking at mobile phone applications, commonly known as apps.

What the next generation has to hold only the future knows.

Right now, let's get started on showing you "The New Marketing Basics".

We're going to show you the basics on how to position your business with the best of the new marketing. We will show you where to go to find the answers if we don't have them here. We realize that we can try as hard as we want, but we are not the only answer to marketing.

What we offer here comes from more than 50 years in marketing and more than 12 years in Internet Marketing experience.
We are on the leading edge of New Marketing every day.

We're going to give you examples on how to tie it all together, so that you can increase your sales and the number of customers you have come to your store or website.

This book was written in chapters. That doesn't mean that they have to be read in order.
Each chapter is meant to be separate so that they can be read in any order.

We give you "the New Marketing Basics" as a guide to get the most **marketing** your **business** can afford.

Let's Go!

PS: We <u>were</u> going to have a check list available in this book. Time was cruel to us, and you will have to go to the check list marketing site (<u>www.checklist-marketing.com</u>) for your FREE check list.

Bill and Thom

<u>www.theNewMarketingBasics.com</u>

(Disclaimer)
<u>Make no promises, Tell no lies!</u>

As much as we would love to think that everyone who follows the advice in "The New Marketing Basics" will become fabulously wealthy by result, the truth is that we can't promise that will happen for you.

We can't guarantee that you will actually read the book, follow our suggestions to the letter, or handle your business in a professional manner that will make customers flock to your company.

We do want YOU to succeed with whatever you do and we hope that you have gained knowledge and have continued success by reading our book.

So here is the nitty-gritty legal statement.

<u>Legal Notices and Disclaimer</u>

THE FOLLOWING TERMS AND CONDITIONS APPLY:
While every attempt has been made to verify information provided, neither Thom Leonard nor Bill Davis, nor any ancillary party, assumes any responsibility for errors, omissions, or contradictory interpretation of the subject matter here in.

Any perceived slights of specific people or organizations are unintentional.

To the fullest extent permitted by applicable laws, in no event shall "The New Marketing Basics", agents or suppliers be liable for damages of any kind or character, including without limitation any compensatory, incidental, direct, indirect, special, punitive, or consequential damages, loss of use, loss of data, loss of income or profit, loss of or damage to property, claims of third parties, or other losses of any kind or character, even if "The New Marketing Basics" has been advised of the possibility of such damages or losses, arising out of or in connection with the use of "The New Marketing Basics" or any website or business with which it is linked.

In other words, if you read this book and put it and what you learned on a shelf in your room / house, you stand a very good chance of not succeeding.

ACKNOWLEDGMENTS

Need to thank everyone that has been a part of our lives over the years as they in an indirect way, have been a part of us having the knowledge to write this book. A special thanks to one Internet Marketer who gave us the idea for this book and without his push we never would have started.

We want to Thank Createspace for the platform to share our thoughts.

1
THE NEW BASICS OF MARKETING

When most people think of marketing the first thing that pops into their head is an advertisement. This leads many people to believe that marketing and advertising is actually the same thing.

They are not.

Here is the definition of "marketing" according to Wikipedia's online dictionary:

> Marketing is "the process by which companies create customer interest in goods or services."

And here is the definition of "advertising" according to Wikipedia:

> "Advertising is a form of communication intended to persuade an audience (viewers, readers or listeners) to purchase or take some action upon a product, ideas, or services."

You can see by those definitions, marketing is much broader than advertising. Advertising is actually part of marketing. But it's not the only part of marketing. Sure, advertising is a major part of marketing, but it isn't even the majority of marketing. Don't ever make the mistake of confusing advertising with marketing. The two terms are not interchangeable and marketing is much larger than advertising, more now than ever and continues to grow in scope.

Advertising is a big part of marketing, but it's far from being the only part. Marketing is so much more. Therefore, in order to be successful in your marketing efforts you have to concentrate on much more than one advertising method.

Examples of advertising at work would be newspaper advertising, yellow page advertising, and magazine advertising. Handouts that you have your name imprinted on would be advertising, too.

Examples of marketing would be how you use the handouts that you had your name imprinted on, what method you use to give them to your customer or potential customer. This would also include posting on Facebook, Digg, and MySpace, LinkedIn, twitter or any other social marketing site.

The typical way of utilizing social marketing sites is to offer a discount that the customer is able to verbally ask for because of an e-mail that they got today or they saw it posted on your Facebook fan page. We will be covering all of these and more in upcoming chapters of this book.

Yes all these are different types of marketing avenues that you can take. It is all about boosting your bottom line by using marketing methods that are tried and true but also outside the box.

As a matter of fact, you might find that out-of-the-box marketing methods work better for you. What they say about marketing and advertising: Start by split testing your market, and split test it again. Most will say that split testing should be an ongoing process, I agree.

Split testing is used for a variety of reasons: To find the best price to sell a product for, the best name, the best type of package to sell the product in, among many others.

By split testing you can find out a lot of different information about your product and how the consumer views your product and how they might use it. Talking to customers that use your product have they found new uses for it? (Tip: Listening to your customers, they might suggest a new product for you and that is money in your pocket.)

Marketing also is the vehicle you drive, the clothes you wear, your customer service methods, right down to how you answer phone calls.

What is the first impression that potential customers get of you?

- How you look.
- How you answer questions.
- How you answer the phone.
- Are you on time?
- How you handle billing.
- What your website says or doesn't say.
- Be positive and cheerful.

This is just a short list of things that your customers will think of and about you on that first meeting.

The methods in which you can connect to your customer have changed dramatically over the last decade; there are more methods at your disposal to start with. We will cover as many of these as we can. Rest assured, as new marketing methods come to the forefront, we will update the material in this book as well as on the website as quickly as possible.

I think you can see that there are a lot of different aspects that go into marketing.

In fact, everything you do is part of your marketing efforts. Sure, marketing is the mailing you do once a year, once a week, once a month or it might even be the phone call you make to see if your past customers need your services this year.

We can carry it a step further by saying that marketing is part of your brand and how you brand yourself is your one of your keys to your marketing strategy. We will be covering branding in this book as well.

We will be delving into social marketing, along with the tried and true newspaper ads, yellow page ads, weekly publication ads, email campaigns and more.

Here is a short list of social media that is available to us today.

<u>Facebook</u> is number one. As they say, 800 million people can't be wrong. It is really hard to brush them aside as they are here adding e-mail to their mix. Some people seemed to measure their social self-worth based on how may Facebook friends they have.
Facebook also caters to businesses by offering **fan pages**, and that's what we're going to be talking about in this book.

<u>MySpace</u> started before Facebook but has been overtaken by Facebook by leaps and bounds. There still may be a place in your marketing plan to cover MySpace. Consequently, we will cover a little bit of MySpace.

<u>Twitter</u> is the 140 character bluebird on the block. A lot of people made money with twitter and there's reason to think that many more could. Twitter popularity seems to be on the downward trend (especially when compared to Facebook), but millions of folks use it daily, including many celebrities like Ashton Kutcher, Kim Kardashian, and Alyssa Milano. We will be offering more information about twitter in the book.

This is a list of the big three in social media. We will cover a number of other social media sites as well, such as <u>Delicious, StumbleUpon, Digg, Reddit, Xomba, Mashable</u> and of course <u>YouTube and LinkedIn</u>.

We will attempt to point you the direction of tools, tips and more on each of these social sites. We will attempt to cover the high points and the low points of each one.

Now don't get us wrong: All the old techniques still work but they're not working as well and as often as we would like them to.
Most customers that have mobile phones are moving into the smart phone category. You might what to ask, what does that mean?
You will find that old marketing methods aren't working as well and Facebook as well as other social media are growing in leaps and bounds. To us, that means we need to move toward the marketing methods that are working, sometimes, whether we want to or not.

In closing of chapter one, *after years of almost exclusive focus on media companies, the Internet has made public relations public again, and put you in control of as much or as little as you want.*

By now you are on Facebook or some other social network and if you are not there you should start. It won't hurt you at all, it will help you communicate with your customers.

www.theNewMarketingBasics.com

2
TIME TO START YOUR BUSINESS PLAN

Why do you need a Business Plan?

The example might be you taking a trip to the grocery store. You know you're going to go for milk, eggs, and butter—you have a plan that's to get the milk, eggs, and butter. You always make a list when you go to the store. It doesn't matter if it's 3 items or 10 items—always make a list (a plan)! That way, you know you're going to get home with everything that you were supposed to get.

Business is no different. In fact, it is far **more important** to devise a plan for your business than it is to make a grocery list. It needs to be a **written plan;** it is not sufficient to have a plan in your mind. If you don't have a written plan it is highly probable that you won't hold yourself accountable to any plan. But if you write it down, then the plan will actually motivate you and keep you on track.

So how do you start?

Here is where you look at what am I going to sell or what service am I going to offer.
This is where you start.
Once this decision is made your path should be the following.

Know your market: is the mantra here.
Any good business man will tell you that the first thing you do is find out,

Who is my:
1:     target audience and why?
2:     how am I going to market to them? The sales process. How much profit can I make and how much do I need to make?
3:     where should the business be? Location, a Mall, a Strip Mall, main street, or where are my customers going to want to find me?
4:     what is my proposition – what are the key elements of your product or service – how are you going to deliver your product.
5:     implementation of your plan.
6:     review.
7:     revised and back to number one.

At first glance it may seem simple, it is meant to be a short list of what your business plan should be. There is really a lot more that goes into a business plan but this will get you started. We really suggest that you get a book about the business plan and follow whichever one that you prefer. A business plan is a whole book in it's self.

On the simple side, let's see who our target audience is.

You can start off by saying or asking where are your customers currently looking and shopping?
How do you figure this out?

By using a keyword search tool, whether you want to market your product online or off-line, the Internet provides some great resources to help you find and understand your customers and how they are searching for looking for your product or service. Begin with a single word or short phrase (2 or 3 words) to describe your product or service, and then expand into the long tail phrase (4 to 8 key words) that might be used to describe your product or service when searching for your product or service.
(Sorry for the double speak) Start by visiting the free Google keyword tool

at:

https://adwords.google.com/select/**KeywordTool**External

Other keyword tools:

free**keywords**.wordtracker.com

Micro Niche Finder at http://1thin.com/MNF

A great tool that I personally use.

http://www.keyworddiscovery.com/search.html

http://www.seochat.com/seo-tools/keyword-suggestions-google/

tools.digitalpoint.com/tracker.php

http://www.wordstream.com/keyword-search-tool

Which one of the keyword search tools you prefer is up to you, there is a lot more that I have not mentioned here.

The newly released (beginning 2011) Google Wonderwheel (free) is one of the best planning tools you can use.

For finding the general scope of the market, and finding related markets. You probably don't realize how your products can tie together until you see something that shows you in print and the Wonderwheel does just that, graphically.

Simply search Google (from a Google search page for best results) for a keyword or phrase and then look alongside the left-hand navigation pane for Wonderwheel (Free). Click it and study the results.

It might even be in your best interests to try multiple keyword search tools to see what different results you might get;

Check at http://www.bing.com/toolbox/webmaster for tools on Bing dot com and Yahoo has a number of sites for tools so here goes the list for them;

https://siteexplorer.search.yahoo.com/

http://tools.search.yahoo.com/about/forsiteowners.html

http://help.yahoo.com/l/us/yahoo/search/indexing/webmaster-01.html

(if you type this one in the dash(-01.html) is included as it is shown)

http://tools.search.yahoo.com/about/

http://help.yahoo.com/l/us/yahoo/search/webmaster/

http://www.digitalpurview.com/yahoo-webmaster-tools/
http://www.search.yahoo.com/info/submit.html to submit your site to Yahoo.

This could help broaden your scope of your total market by helping you see markets that you didn't see before.

Now if this list doesn't confuse you about all of the search engine tools that are available then check out this sites;

http://www.searchenginegenie.com/seo-tools.htm.

To get the most value from your keyword tool, you are going to pick what key words best describe your product or service.

This will then give you results of actual searches that people have made over the last 30 days (with most key word tools) using your keywords or phrase.

This is the same basic method that you would use creating your USP/elevator pitch, more on that later.

What is different here is that you are trying to locate where your customers are and how they are searching for your product or service.

Now that we know our customers, how are we going to reach them?

We go more into this in the chapter about Marketing. While you are working on your business plan take a look at the Chapter on Marketing to see what you think and feel would be the best marketing plan. Then come back here after you know how you intend to start marketing to your customers.

Where we locate our business?

For some this can be your hardest decision, because you are trying to save money to open your business.

The easiest I think is to start your business in your home and spin off into a location after you get input from your current customers and have the cash flow to warrant the move. That doesn't always work, as some businesses must have a bricks and mortar location.

A point that needs to be noted here, is that in Real Estate the mantra is three words "LOCATION – LOCATION – LOCATION", this is one that I have been reminded of through my whole life as my mother was a Real Estate Broker in Silicon Valley and Property Manager as well and even there the mantra is the same.

Now that I said all of that, You need to decide how much you need to worry about the location of your business. I know that not all businesses have the optimum location and to some it really doesn't matter.

Example might be a supply house for the retail businesses around town or local delivery service. These could be in some business park or warehouse somewhere in your town. Now a barber or beauty shop should be in a well trafficked area. This is the general thought on this type of business.

How are you going to deliver your product to your customers?

This is all about your product and how your customer takes possession of your product or service. Cash and carry to me is the best deal that you can offer you customer. They pay for the product or service and take delivery of either now.

When going into a customer's home to deliver a product that they have purchased from you, the sale is not complete until the customer signs off on the delivery / install.

Keep in mind that if you deliver your product then you need to make your delivery / setup the best that you possibly can. This can mean that you include the delivery and installation is included in the purchase price.

www.theNewMarketingBasics.com

3
BEGIN WITH A MESSAGE
YOUR ELEVATOR PITCH / USP

It doesn't matter how small or large your goals may be—you always need a plan. In this case you need a marketing plan as part of your business plan.

How do you begin to put together a marketing plan? Well it all has to start with a message.

In order to properly put together a marketing plan you must first have to figure out your message. You need to decide on what you want your business to say to people.

This message will be laced through everything you do. The message needs to grab the attention of people and make them want to use your business. The message also has to set you apart from other people.

This message is called your "elevator pitch or USP"; some say it should be as short as 30 seconds and should take no more than 2 minutes to convey. (It was given this name because you should be able to tell someone exactly what you do while you're in an elevator together. That is about all of the time that you will have.)

We lean towards 30 seconds or less, which is about 90 words. Many people won't listen for more than 15 seconds; if you're a fast talker then you'll rock.

Fact is, the vast majority of companies don't have this simple but essential positioning statement in place. They never took the time to define their business model in clear concise words. In fact, many companies set up shop, open the doors, and hope for the best.

You're going to change that. Most businesses don't have a true focus. Your Elevator Pitch / USP can form the foundation for your entire business. It can give you something to strive for every day to be the best you possibly can be for your customer.

So how do you determine what your USP is?

This is where you turn detective, break out the Yellow Pages, and start reading to see what your competition is saying about their own business.

This means you have to make a list of their USPs for each and every competitor that you have. With this list you can now determine what areas that your competition is weak in or where you can excel above your competition.

You may find that your competition is all saying about the same thing in their ads, if they're all saying the same thing how can any 1 business hope to be successful with their ads? They may think they can, but logic has it, not likely.

This is where you have to think outside the box: Take your competition's USPs and see how you can make yours better. What kind of twist can you put to what your competition is doing that makes yours better?

Look at a national company and what they did. The car company used the slogan, "We Try Harder". It was simple but it worked; now that's outside the box.

Some of the most successful USPs include:

- Dominoes Pizza promising to deliver your pizza in 30 min. or less or the pizza is free.

- FedEx; promising to absolutely deliver a product, overnight.

- The Subway chain positioning itself as a fast food alternative that will help you lose weight.

- American Express credit cards; claiming that they are accepted everywhere in the world.

A great USP can be anything about your business that provides a benefit to your customer that other businesses don't do. But it doesn't always have to be a benefit.

A great example of this is the McDonald's fast food chain restaurants putting on all their signs just below the "M" that they have served over 1 billion hamburgers or whatever the number may be right now. This actually feeds in to the herd mentality that exists in society.

People love to follow others, so a person seeing that so many other people have eaten in a restaurant will be more likely to eat at that restaurant. Again this worked, again thinking outside the box.

Okay, I get it, now you say it's time to sit down and create your own USP. How should you start, what questions should you USP answer?

"Why should a person choose my business over any other business?"

Simply put, your USP / Elevator Pitch should answer that question.

That's the importance of the USP. And it can make the difference how easy success comes to you. A great USP can put you well on the way to success, early success at that. I'm not going to say that you're going to be the next Yahoo or Google but you just might be the next Zappos.

Above all don't forget to ask your friends what they think your USP should be.

Building Your Elevator Pitch.

To us the USP isn't just **part** of your elevator pitch. We believe that it is the **heart** of your elevator pitch.

Taking the time to write your elevator pitch forces you to find the focus of your business, so let's start **with the precious facts** that you may want to think about when creating your elevator pitch. Most of these won't come as any surprise to you.

This is a good time to be reminded of them:

1. Customers like honesty.

2. Customers will be loyal to a business that they trust.

3. Customers like a good job done as fast as possible.

4. Customers want authenticity, not spin.

5. Customers want participation, not propaganda.

6. Customers like the professional look of businesses.

7. Customers like to be treated professionally as well.

8. Customer service should be your number one priority at all times.

9. Not all potential customers are the same; therefore, not all potential customers will react the same way to your elevator pitch.

10. If somebody takes your pitch as being odd or funny or peculiar, don't you be offended, try to use that to your benefit.

11. Do your best to not offend your customer. If your pitch is one that can be misinterpreted, then maybe you should try for something not so questionable. Might be a good time to rethink your elevator pitch.

One example of how people might have different likes and dislikes is if your pitch is attractive to teenagers it may not be attractive to the elderly.

This is clearly the case of you need to make your pitch geared towards the consumer that you want to target. Sounds simple, right?

So let's get started.
These are the questions you need to answer within that first 15-30 seconds of meeting someone who may inquire as to what you do:

1. Who is it about? What customers can you serve?

2. What is your specialty? What do you do?

3. What can you do to solve their problem? What are your solutions that can help eliminate a problem?

4. Why are you better than the competition? How are you different?

5. What does a customer need to do to take advantage of your business? In other words, tell customers how they can use your services; ask for their business.

Now put it all together. Write it all in a paragraph format and read it to yourself make adjustments by trying different words until it sounds right.

Once you're happy with it, read it to your friends and colleagues. Read it people who have no idea what you do and ask them if your elevator pitch makes it clear.

Now the pitch:

- Identify who you are and what your specialty is. For example, *"Hello my name is Frank and I am a businessman specializing in widgets."*
  Remember your USP?

- Describe your specialty in more detail. It needs to do more than that, though; it also needs to identify the problem that exists and how you solve that problem. Include what you do to solve it.

- How you are different from your competition, what makes you different? Why you are better? Set your business apart from your competition.

- Tell your prospect what to do next, be specific, and supply a strong call to action.

A couple of last tips: Don't say too much. Be quick and concise. Use complete sentences. Be clear and simple. Dumb it down. Seriously, That's it.

Second, dumb it down. Seriously, get rid of the jargon and catch phrases, even the ones you think everybody should know. They don't. ***People not in your field don't know the industry vernacular or verbiage, so take it out. You want it to be at sixth grade level; your message has to be easy to understand.***

This project is far more important than you might think. It forms the basis for everything else you do.

To recap: The points your elevator pitch should address.

- Number one identifies you.

- Number two tells your prospects what problem(s) you solve.

- Number three tells your prospect why you are better than your competition.

- Number four gives a call to action!

Make adjustments as you see fit to refine it over time. In fact, construct 3-4 elevator pitches and test them. See which ones get the best responses. Test and tweak. That's a term you'll hear throughout this book. **Test and Tweak.**

www.theNewMarketingBasics.com

4
MARKETING PLAN

Now this is where it gets tricky, now you know what your customers are searching for, you need to determine how to best reach them. This is part of your marketing plan where your choices are many and generally your budget is slim.

So how are you going to market to your consumer? Use the Internet to market to your customers or are you going to use conventional marketing methods (newspaper, Yellow Pages, Pennysaver, handing out flyers / coupons) or are you going to use multiple methods, which is best, if you can afford it.

If you're an Internet business let's face it the only thing you need to do is advertise on the Internet. However there have been some Internet marketers that have had some success with postcards, radio and or podcasts, this is also a good choice and video has made its way as the choice of the leading internet marketers. YouTube videos are not the only host for your videos. Keep in mind that there is a number of video sharing sites now so YouTube is not a must have.

Remember that the most of larger retailers advertise every day, week and month. And they advertise in many different ways.

Once you have decided which method or methods you're going to use to start with, you need to set yourself an obtainable goal of number of sales that you think you can make. This does not have to be an exact count, just a starting point.

You want to keep this goal realistic but you also want to make yourself reach for it. In other words, you want to set a goal that will force you to work hard to achieve it but not cause you to become frustrated because you can't reach it and quit.

As you go forward you might have to readjust your goal higher or lower depending on how the year is going. Don't be depressed if you have to lower your goal; there's no shame in that. The shame would be not adjusting it and punishing yourself because you missed your goal.

This might be a good time to mention, as you implement one strategy of advertising your product or service, you want to keep adding other methods as time goes along to increase your market penetration. Start all campaigns on the same day of the week. Most businesses have a typical daily or weekly cycle that makes this starting time important.

Now that you have implemented your marketing plan, the first time, it is now time to review what you have done and how successful you have been, so that you can make the changes that need to be made to your marketing campaign so that it will be more successful in the future.

Might make a footnote here, don't wait till the end of the year to make changes to your marketing plan, look at what's going on in the first month, or week. If you make changes often be sure not to make too drastic of changes that often unless one of your methods bombs totally and it may take days to see a total bomb.

Keep changes as small as possible, save your major changes for the end of the week or end of the month, so that you are starting off the new month or week with a new plan/method.
This will help keep you on track for reaching your ultimate goal by the end of the year.

Keep track (records, records, records) of what and how you are doing. This is the best way of seeing how well you are doing and what method is working best. It is important that you keep records, so that you know exactly what is working or not.

Your marketing plan has to go much deeper, it should be every detail including what you need to do each day and what your goals are and how you'll achieve those goals.

The better records that you keep will help you make money faster, and sure you have to implement your plan to make it work more than anything.

Don't just plan, DO the PLAN!   **Test and Tweek.**

www.theNewMarketingBasics.com

5
A WINNING STRATEGY

Time to get serious. Now we're talking money. It's what we like to talk about, so get ready!

When putting together your marketing plan you need to consider how much money you have to spend, if any, and/or how you will spend that money.

Remember, there are dozens—if not hundreds—of places to spend your marketing dollars and all players are ready, willing, and able to take your money. So beware.

You need to think about the free methods that are available to market your business and then the plan which will work best for you. As with all marketing tactics, you need to keep in mind your target customers.

When you test your market and marketing strategies to see what works for you, make sure that you plan each attempt for the same length of time. That way if something doesn't work over the same time that another strategy did you will have a good basis for each test. For the ones that don't work change it a bit and retry. Once you open for business and start advertising it then becomes

Test and Tweak.

And remember that just because it worked (or didn't) doesn't mean it will (or won't) work next week, next month, or next year. Be open-minded.

Tweak and Test, see what works.

However, all that said, knowing what has worked in the past, use it again, and refrain from using the "duds" in any big way until you test and tweak it in a small trial.

Keep records of what you did so that you can keep what works and what doesn't. This will be more important as time goes on.

Test and Tweak.

Now is a good time where we must point out that a marketing plan is absolutely essential if you want to be successful. Sadly only about 1% of all private business owners usually make a detailed marketing plan and they don't even realize how much business they are losing without one.

Research points to the fact that businesses that have a marketing plan outperform those who don't have a marketing plan by about 30%.

So if one business is making $40,000 a year without a marketing plan, that business could make as much as $52,000+ with a marketing plan.

Is it worth $12,000 a year (or more) to you to invest a few hours in a marketing plan?

If your answer is "No," give this book to someone else and do whatever you're going to do.

However, if your answer is "Yes," then keep reading. We like you. You're a sharp cookie.

We would say that your chances are better than 30% if you start with a business plan/marketing plan and stick to it.

We both have had personal experience where we have had no basic plan of anything but the first sale and the next few sales. That's part of the hazards of thinking that you can do it without a plan.

To be most effective, the plan has to be formalized, usually in written form, as a formal marketing plan.

The essence of the process is that it moves from general to the specific, from the vision, to the mission, to the goals, to the objectives of the organization, then down to the individual action plans for each part of the marketing program. This part is going to explain how you're going to get your customers to buy your product and/or services.

The plan will then include sections detailing your:

- product and/or services and your unique selling position

- USP

- pricing strategy

- sales/Distribution Plan

- advertising and promotion plan

A marketing plan is just that important; it is the most important part of your business plan.

If you have no sales then you have no business. Period.

www.theNewMarketingBasics.com

6
BRANDING

So we make it perfectly clear what branding really is, here's a short definition: it is the purpose to get people to recall your company/product/service from memory.

The ultimate aim is to get people to trust you more than the competition, and to think of you and your business before they think of the competition.

This should have been part of the USP/elevator pitch. However, we thought there should be a section just devoted to branding. It's very tough to pin down one exact definition for branding. Sure, you can look it up online or in a dictionary but it will still be tough to come up with just one definition.

What you need to know is branding is the way a product or service and even the entire company is presented and the way people see that product or company.

So branding is the slogan, USP/elevator pitch, the colors, trademarks, symbols, type of product or service sold and anything else that goes along with the presentation of a product or company.

A good example is Nike; they have done an outstanding job with branding. Everyone knows the Nike swoosh symbol. You're also probably familiar with the "just do it" slogan.

For years Nike is published a lot of posters with athletes and dark backgrounds. That was part of their branding too. It was dark and edgy. It was hip. To add to this brand Nike loves to combine music, cool scenes, and popular athletes.

All the athletes that Nike sponsors are also part of their brand. In fact, sponsors are a major part of branding for any company. That's why it is so important for the athletes not to get in trouble. An athlete that gets in trouble is a direct reflection on the sponsoring company. That can be good or bad. But when an athlete does something great, that gives a great boost to the product and/or company.

The 2008 summer games showed just how important branding really is, and how branding works.

Many of the best swimmers for the United States were sponsored by Nike. However, a rival brand of swimsuit, Speedo, had invented a swimsuit that allowed a swimmer to swim through the water with little or no resistance. Therefore a swimmer wearing a Speedo suit automatically had an advantage over a swimmer wearing a Nike suit. So Nike made the business decision to allow all of their sponsored swimmers to wear Speedo suits.

The decision by Nike was completely based on branding. Sure, they hurt their brand a little by not having their sponsored swimmers wearing Nike suits while they were in the water during the Olympics.

However, by allowing their swimmers to wear Speedo suits, Nike was giving their swimmers every opportunity to win medals at the Olympics. Winning medals at the Olympics would boost the popularity of their athletes and thus increase brand awareness for Nike.

So Nike gave up a little branding in the short term in order to gain a lot more attention in the future.

Branding is also how you treat your customers.

Just as you're always marketing, you should be aware that most of the time you are also building your brand. So make sure that you have a very clear picture for what you want your brand to be and make sure you include branding in your marketing plan.

So how do you build this elusive brand?

The first thing you need to know is that you don't actually perceive your brand, everyone else does. Therefore, you need to build your brand trying to see things through the eyes of your customers.

Next thing you need to know is that the best brands tap into people's emotions. Also, as with marketing (remember USP/elevator pitch), you want to be unique with your brand. Set yourself apart from your competition with your brand.

To build a brand you'll need to develop it, define your message, and then market it. Once that's done you'll present your brand visually, verbally, and through your actions.

This part is very important that you make sure that all of your promotional material, letterhead, business cards, brochures, signage, etc. has the right logo, the right slogan, and the right colors.

Make sure your clothing, the logo on your truck, and everything else matches as well. This seems easy but you would be surprised how many people don't do it.

Don't forget one of the oldest methods around today; that would be inexpensive merchandise like hats, golf balls, or T-shirts with your logo printed on it for handing out at special events or for the holidays.

Keep in mind that nowadays your brand is extended to Facebook, twitter, MySpace, Digg, LinkedIn, and any of the other social media sites that you might think of.

It would be in your better interest to embrace these new technologies as best as you possibly can.

You don't have to have all of them but start slow, build one site at a time, then over time you will expand into as many as you possibly can.

You can also add to your branding by having your own blog and asking customers to post on it as well as being a guest poster on other blogs that would be relevant to your business.

You could start a discussion board or forum for your business, start an outreach program for your customers, you could have a weekly pod cast, you could do ratings and reviews of products that you sell, as well as being a sponsor of a local event.

All of this represents the brand you are trying to build.

Here is a list of best branding tips for your business.
1. Develop a memorable USP/elevator pitch.
2. Regularly write and issue press releases to the media.
3. Regularly write and post to your website/fan page.
4. Participate in at least two national and or local industry conferences annually.
5. Have your own weekly, daily, monthly newsletter.
6. Be known for your niche expertise.
7. Participate in professional internship programs.
8. Develop a tip sheet for your customers.
9. Develop an outreach program for your customers.
10. Discover the strengths of your business and how to use them.
11. Create an experience for the customer.
12. Be aware of following trends, good and bad.

This is just a short list of ways that you can help brand your business, often referred to as the goodwill portion of your business. Your brand is intangible and has nothing at all to do with any real estate, inventory or vehicles in your fleet.

It does refer to the reputation behind your company's name and logo.

www.theNewMarketingBasics.com

7

MARKETING METHODS & TECHNIQUES

In the first couple of chapters we look at the importance of marketing and having a marketing plan. We also looked at the USP/elevator speech or pitch, and branding.

All of this has to be part of your marketing plan. However, none will help you with the specifics for how you'll need to market your business. In this chapter we'll get into specifics.

Part of your marketing business may be in newspapers, the yellow pages, and other places around your service area, Pennysaver or other local newspapers. You can also market on the Internet and you can use some unique marketing techniques. These unique ways include free ways to get publicity.

Advertising in Newspapers

Placing ads in newspapers is not nearly as effective as it once was. Every single day fewer people are reading newspapers and even fewer are actually looking at the classified ads in newspapers. However, newspaper ads are still very important for local businesses; therefore, you may feel that you need to use this advertising medium. You're about to discover how easy that it can provide a boost to your business. The tips that we're going to cover are primarily for local newspapers or trade magazines that have a classified section at generally very reasonable prices for these ads.

Here are 10 tips that you always want to follow when placing newspaper ads:

1.   ADVERTISE CONSISTENTLY: One problem with advertising in papers is that you could be missing 50% or more potential customers on any given day. They could be away for the day, they might be too busy to read the paper, their dog might've chewed it up, etc. Don't place an ad one time and expect it to bring customers flocking to your business. It won't work, (this statement is a general one at that, newspaper ads just might work for some. Try them in moderation.)

To avoid this problem, place your ad as consistently as possible. If you're running a larger ad (and they are most effective) then you want to try to run the ad at least once a week for a few weeks. If you're listing your ad in the classified section then you want to make sure it runs just about every single day for a few weeks or months.

To see what I mean, look in the classified section of any paper and see what ads are running on a daily basis. You may see ads from auto dealers and real estate offices that run on a daily basis.

Running an ad for more than a month is typically considered institutional advertising. Much like large corporations do in their weekly ads and over time they do work, but it takes time and money—mostly money.

2.   THINK about the DAY and the TIME of YEAR:
Different ads for different products and services will work better on certain days in certain times of the year. The days you run an ad and the time of year you run more ads should all be thought through carefully and made part of your marketing plan. As you place ads and keep track of their performance you'll be able to discover which days' work best and when the best time of year is to run such ads. Here is a good time to look at your competition and see what they are doing.

This is important: Always be aware of what your competition is doing and either a) do it better, b) do it different or c) do it more.

Here is a quick overall review for each day of the week:

SATURDAY

Many advertisers believe this is a bad day to advertise your business. But actually it's a good day to advertise. First, there is less competition on Saturdays since most businesses stay away from this day. Secondly many people wake-up on Saturday and think about the things they have to do around the house. If they see your ad they just might call you instead of doing it themselves.

SUNDAY

The Sunday paper has a lot of readers. But there is a lot of competition too. However, it's a good day to advertise, especially for financial and business-related businesses.

MONDAY

A lot of men read the paper on Monday because of the recap on the weekend sports.

TUESDAY

This is a good day to advertise for financial businesses and business-related businesses.

WEDNESDAY

This is the best day for food-related and health businesses. Most grocery stores change their ads on this day.

THURSDAY

This is a pretty good day to advertise. One of the reasons is because people begin to look for weekend events on this day. This includes people looking for garage sales.

FRIDAY

Again, people begin looking forward to the weekend and they start thinking about what they have to do. Maybe they want to go to a music festival on Saturday but they also need to clean their carpets. They see your ad and call you so they can go to the Festival and have you clean their carpets for them.

3.   SIZE and POSITION is EVERYTHING: The size of your ad and where your ad is located is as important as or perhaps even more important than what your ad actually says. First of all, advertisers used to clamor to be on the right hand side of the newspaper. This is because that's the side of the paper that people see first as they turn from page to page. However, studies show that just as many people read the paper from back to front as read it from front to back. Therefore, it doesn't really matter what side of the paper your ad is on.

What is important is that your ad be placed above the fold. In other words, you want your ad to appear on the top half of the paper.

It's also important to try and get your ad listed in the main news section of the newspaper. You also want to be as close to the front of the section as you possibly can get it.

Finally, it's important that your ad dominate the page that it is on. Usually this means that the ad is 12 inches high and at least five columns wide. In fact, an ad that is more than 50% of a page in width and height is every bit as effective as an ad that is a full page.

4.   COLOR is BEST: Color ads draw more attention and converts (media will turn potential customers into actual paying customers) far better than black and white ads. Colored ads are more expensive but the extra cost is well worth it. Color will help you catch the reader's eye.

If you can't afford to run a full color ad then simply using one color to highlight or accent the ad (with the rest being lack of white) is also effective. Just make sure you carefully choose that one color.

5.   DON'T LET the PAPER DESIGN YOUR AD for you: If you let the newspaper create your ad for you then it's probably going to look like every other ad that's run in the paper. Remember you want your ad and your business to stand apart from your competition. If you make your own ad, look at your competition and make yours different in some way, color, type font, color picture or some other way to make your ad stand out from the crowd.

If possible, pay to have your ad professionally done by someone who has a lot of experience with designing newspaper ads. The money you'll spend will be well worth it. **But whatever you do, don't let the newspaper design your ad**.

6.   **TEST YOUR AD (and track it, too):**   Make sure you test all the ads you run anywhere. (This is actually something you should do with all of your marketing.) You want to see how much your business is helped with each and every ad you place. And you want to track what happens with all your ads too.

One of the best and easiest ways to do this is to include a coupon with the ad. The coupon can be of any type of offer just make sure it's a good enough offer to encourage people to use it. Then when people do use the coupon you'll know which ad caused them to decide to do business with you.

You should test the days of the week you run your ad, where you run the ad in the newspaper, any special offers you make, and the headlines you use. You won't know what works best until you test it and see what resonates with customers.

7.   **MAKE GOOD USE of SPACE:** You're paying for the space in the newspaper so make sure you use up all the space. Also, be sure you tell the reader everything they need to know about your business so that they can hire you. Tell them who you are, what you do, why they should hire you, and how they can get in touch with you. An expanded elevator pitch/USP.

8.   **IT'S all about the HEADLINE:** The headline on your ad will make or break you. The headline has to hook the reader and get the reader to look at the rest of the advertisement. If the headline is good the ad will be

effective (as long as the rest of the ad is decent). If the headline is bad then you won't get any business from the ad, regardless of how great the rest of the ad copy might be.

Headlines are so important that there is an entire section on how to write them in a couple of pages. This section will teach you how to write killer headlines and it'll also give you examples of great headlines.

9.   MAKE it NEWSWORTHY: It's obvious that people are reading the newspaper for the news. Therefore, try to make your ad related to the news in some way. That's not always the easiest thing to do for some businesses, but it's not impossible. For example, during a warm and dry summer you might write something like: "Has the dry summer left your Windows dusty and dirty? We'll clean them for you...."

At least try to tie your ad into what's happening in the news. Your ad will convert much better if you can do it effectively.

10. GIVE it TIME to WORK: Newspaper ads usually don't work overnight. Many people will cut out an ad and leave it on their refrigerator until they need it. Then when they need what you're offering they will call you.

So don't expect your ad to work right away. And certainly don't feel like your ad was a failure if it doesn't grab a lot of business for you in the first week or so.

This actually brings us right back to the first tip –
"ADVERTISE CONSISTENTLY". You want to keep advertising in order to make it effective. So make sure you give it plenty of time to work before you declare it a failure.

There you have 10 tips to follow in order to place an ad in the newspaper. Again, you have the option of placing a small ad in the classified section or placing a larger ad and more expensive ad somewhere else in the newspaper. Most of the above tips can be applied to either size ads.

If you are listing your ad in the classified section then you want to make sure your headline tells readers what service you're offering. Usually people will scan the classifieds looking for a particular type of ad. So make sure your headline catches their eye. No matter what type of ad you're running, you will need killer headlines.

KILLER HEADLINES

Before you even start to write your headline, you need to remind yourself the three main functions of a good headline. They are to grab attention, to speak directly to the intended audience, and to deliver a complete message.

An effective headline has to grab the potential customer's attention. If the headline doesn't grab people's attention then that entire piece of marketing will be a complete failure because nobody will ever buy anything from you.

An effective headline also has to be written directly to the intended audience. Obviously you wouldn't use the same words in a headline for teenagers as you would a headline for the elderly. A great way to make sure you're writing to the right audience is to imagine your ideal customer. Then pretend that you are writing directly to just that one person as if they are standing in front of you.

Finally, your headline needs to deliver a message. You need to give the prospect (potential customer) a reason to keep reading the rest of what's written. You need a strong message that will get the person to take time to keep reading your copy and to eventually become a customer.

The 4 U's

When you actually begin crafting a headline, you want to write it so that the 4U's are covered. This means your headline should be unique, useful, ultra-specific, and urgent. If your headline is all of these things then it will do its job.

Here is a quick look at exactly what each one of the 4U's means:

UNIQUE – your headlines need to say something that is different. It can't just be the same old thing or your potential customer will ignore it.

USEFUL – your headline has to have value to the potential reader. You need to give people a reason to be interested in what you're marketing.

ULTRA-SPECIFIC – be as specific as you can with all your headlines. Narrow your message down to just one idea.

URGENT – the key is to get the customer to act right away. So your headline should highlight a benefit that the person will get if they act right away.

There are a couple other keys that you should always remember when you're writing headlines. The first is that you want to tap into the prospect's emotions. (This actually goes along with making the headline useful.) More often than not, people buy based on emotion, so tap into it.

The second key is to always include a major benefit in your headline. This is really easy if you're writing a postcard announcement to a 50% off sale. There's your major benefit. However, if you don't have an obvious benefit then you should sit down and brainstorm all the benefits you offer. Then choose the best one and include that in your headline.

Just remember that you want it to be a benefit. In other words, you want it have direct value for the reader. You do NOT want to simply give a feature of a product.

For example, if you were selling windshield wipers, the best feature of the wiper is that they wipe moisture away from a windshield, right? However, the greatest benefit is that they allow the driver to see and drive safely. Understand the difference? (You sell the ability to see. Not that it wipes the water off the windshield.)

Take the feature of a product or service one step further and write about the benefit it will provide for the potential customer. Also, whenever possible include "Why" and "How" in your headlines.

"How" conveys that you are about to tell the reader something they didn't know about before (and everyone wants to learn something that will improve their life).

"Why" does basically the same thing. It implies that there is a valuable piece of information (or a product or service) that's about to be offered. Here are a couple examples:

"Why you'll never have to clean your own Windows again."

"Stop cleaning your Windows! Here's how…"

Etc.

Another great idea for headlines is asking a question. This is personal and immediately gets the reader thinking of themselves and their own needs. Here are a couple of examples of possible headlines:

"Are you too busy to clean your windows? Now you can spend your time doing the things you love!"

"Are you sick of cleaning your Windows? Now, you don't have to do it ever again."

And here is an example of how you can combine both of the ideas:

"Have you had enough of cleaning your filthy windows? Here's how you can say goodbye to window cleaning forever!"

"Do you want to know how you can stop cleaning your own windows?"

Feel free to "borrow" these headlines or to put your own unique spin on them. You can swipe the above headlines to use as you wish.

In this case, you can use the exact headlines. But for the other headlines you see, you can't take them word for word but you certainly can use them for ideas. In fact, professional copywriters do that all the time. They call it a "swipe." The best copywriters save every good piece of marketing they see into a file that they—appropriately—call a "swipe file."

Every time you see a headline that you like, save it and add it to your own swipe file. I wish someone had told us about this 35+ years ago! We would have a swipe file to end all swipe files. The point is, start one now.

To get you started, here are a few more headlines along with the company that owns the copyright. Feel free to "borrow" the general idea...

"Caught soon enough, early tooth decay can actually be repaired by Colgate." – Colgate

"What in the world is wrong with me?" – Prevention magazine

"Try burning this coupon." – Harshaw chemical (Just kidding, good punch line though.)

"Finally, a Caribbean cruise as good as its brochure." – Norwegian cruise line

ADVERTISING in the Yellow Pages

When someone wants or needs anything done, the first place they used to go to the yellow pages. That used to be the mantra, but from what we have seen in the works that's not going to be forever. For example, watching Thom's children (they range from 31 to 45) deal with a service need reveals that they go to their smart phones and search for what they need.

If you're "old school" and you think you need to have a yellow page ad you want to make sure it stands out from the rest of your competition. And remember to closely monitor your results.

The Yellow Pages has an online campaign going on where looks like they are taking on all comers to this market. Yellow Book, etc.

Here are eight strategies to help your business rise above the competition in the yellow pages:

1.   The Headline is Everything   Just as you discovered with newspaper ads, the headline is very important. In fact, in the yellow pages it's even more important. You need to stand out from the rest of the businesses that are there. The way you rise above the competition is by writing a great headline for your yellow pages ad.

You might think you need to put your business name as the headline but that's not right. In fact you want to put your greatest benefit in the headline. Since you already came up with your USP, this should be very easy to do.

The best headline will include what your business is all about and why people should choose it. Just make sure your business name and phone number is obvious in the ad as well.

2.   Get the biggest ad you can afford   When it comes to the yellow pages bigger is really better. You need to either have a full page spread or even a two page spread. The larger your ad is the more likely you are to attract customers. *In fact, making your ad two times bigger than most other ads will probably net you three or four times more customers.*

Not only is a larger ad easier for a potential customer to find, but it also makes you look larger and more successful. For many people success means that you're good at what you do.

Finally, in many yellow pages the larger ads are put first. Therefore, a larger ad will allow you to be seen first. You will notice that most of the ads are on the top and the outer 2/3s of the page. This is where the eye typically goes when scanning a page.

You need to be careful about not overextending yourself by spending too much on a huge yellow page ad. You certainly don't want to spend all or most of your advertising budget on just the yellow page ad.

3.   Remember selling points and benefits   As with any marketing promotion, you need to make sure you include plenty of selling points and benefits. It won't matter how large your ad is or how great your headline might be if the rest of your copy isn't filled with selling points and benefits. You have to tell potential customers why it makes perfect sense for them to hire you or buy from you.

One of the greatest techniques you can use is to include testimonials. People will trust a third party much more than they'll trust an actual business. So always try to include a couple of testimonials with every ad you run.

Here are a few other strategies dealing with how to build your ad:

- Use a font (type style) that's easy to read

- Include a headshot of yourself

- Use other photographs too. People love photos

- Also include captions under the photos just to make sure they look good in the ad

- Use all the space you have

- Insert a dateline (the year, and the place of your business) in your ad

- Don't use all capital letters unless it's for a short word such as FREE

- Don't be afraid to be different with your ad. Remember, different will help you stand apart from your competition.

4.   Always include an offer   Always include some type of offer with every ad you place. Each ad will have a different offer (it doesn't have to be a big change in the offer just something different). The offer could be 25% off or it could be a free report that you'll send them. *Just make sure you create a good call to action along with the offer.* Ask them to do something—like join your mailing list—so that in this case they take advantage of your offer)

5.   Test your ad first   Your yellow pages ad will run for an entire year. So you want to make sure it's as effective as possible. There's only one way to make sure it's effective—test it beforehand. Start by putting a similar ad in the newspaper a few months before you run your yellow pages ad to see how it does. Then tweak it and test it again. Keep testing until you are happy with how it is doing.
This way you'll get great results for the entire year!

6.   Research the best directory for you and your business
In many cities there is more than one directory. If you can afford to put an ad in all of them that's great and that's what you should do. If not, you need to choose the directory that is best for you.

The best way to really find out which is the better book in your area would be to ask other businesses, your competition, or your next-door neighbor to your business and just ask some friends what they use for looking for a business or service.

7.   Protect your ad.   There are two parts to this idea. The first part is protecting your actual ad from competitors who might try to steal your ideas.
The second is protecting the look of your ad and what it says when the people at the yellow pages try to get you to change it.
When your competitors see how effective your ad is, they are very likely to try to steal it and make a similar ad.

You can protect your ad by simply copyrighting it. You don't need to send it away to get protect it protected either. In fact, your ad is protected under what is called common law copyright. All you have to do is put the following at the bottom of your ad:

"© 2011 your business name."

That will allow you to take someone to court for using your ideas, or slogans.

When you submit your ad to the yellow pages they will probably try to get you to change it. They are used to the ads all looking a certain way. Yours appearing different will almost certainly throw them for a loop. They'll think you don't know what you're doing. But don't listen to them. They don't know your business and almost all of them don't know very much about marketing either. So stick to your own ideas and make them run your ad the way you want it to be run.

8.   Don't forget to track your ad.

Again, as with all your marketing promotions, make sure you track your results.

That way you can improve on your ad for next year.

Another great idea for tracking is to simply tell the customer to ask for a different extension when they call. So in one ad you might put "ask for extension A and in the other ad you might put "ask for extension B." Then you'll know which ad led the customers to call by the extension they request.

This is a very simple method for tracking but there are a number of other simple methods for tracking that you can use. If you have two incoming phone lines, use one for one ad and the other for the other ad. Don't have another phone line? Use a different person's name for each ad.

Before we move on, it needs to be mentioned that there are many other less common publications that you can advertise in also.

One that is often overlooked is a church directory or bulletin. It's usually relatively cheap to advertise in and the credibility you'll earn will make it well worth the money.

When you have your ties in a church bulletin people who go to that church will automatically see you as being associated with the church. This will lead many people to like and trust you right from the beginning.

There may be small papers or magazines in your area that can land you similar results. Just keep your eyes and ears open and realize that there is a lot of value to be gotten from these smaller publications.

While the circulation might be small, your conversion rate could be very high (the number of customers who see your ad and hire you).

Here's one VERY important bit of information that we need to share with you. The yellow pages have been losing ground all around this great nation, for the last few years, and that is because of Facebook, LinkedIn, MySpace, twitter, and more social sites that have gained traction. However from some of the latest tactics that they have employed I would not count them out just yet. They are really getting aggressive toward marketing to the online consumer as well.

The younger generation uses their smart phones and Google or some other search engine to find what they're looking for.

Thom's 30-something children do it that way and I think of them as being normal, so why don't we embrace it? Because it is change and we don't like change. I am here to tell you that this is going to happen if you're there or not. It is your choice.

It has not been an easy transition for me from film cameras to the digital camera, and the phone that comes from being a desk top or wall appliance to this sleek compact computer that is also a phone.

We would tread lightly before we placed an ad in the Yellow Pages, simply because it is too hard to change the ad in the middle of the year if it is not working. After you have a known working ad that you would feel comfortable putting in the Yellow book for a year, by all means do. But make it a proven ad.

There are way too many other less expensive and more effective methods for advertising your business.

Direct mail marketing

Direct mail marketing is sending out any type of mail catalogs, postcards, letters or flyers to potential customers.

Postcards work the best because there's nothing to open so all the mail recipients will automatically see at least part of your message. Postcards are also cheaper to make and cheaper to mail. Post cards are one of the best ways for the small business to experience mail order on the cheap, you can get a good bang for your buck.

It's best if you use your direct mail marketing campaign to announce a special event of some type. (This will be covered later in this chapter) If you don't have a list you can buy a mailing list from one of the many great companies that are out there. A great site for mailing lists is www.directmail.com. You can also compile your own list. (In a couple pages you'll see how you can use a box in other businesses to do this. Then near the end of the chapter you'll see how you can build an e-mail list for e-mail marketing.)

You also want to follow these strategies for your direct mail marketing:

Create the best headline possible.   As with any type of marketing, the **Headline** needs to capture the reader's attention. Use the advice for creating headlines that was discussed earlier in this chapter, and make sure your headline is as great as it can be.

Pick the right image for your postcard.   You should only have one image on the non-address side of your postcard. Don't just choose an image because you think it looks cool. Choose an image that fits with your overall brand and/or the goal of your direct marketing campaign.

Go with one major idea and keep it simple. You have limited space with the postcard and you also have limited time with the reader.

Make sure you focus on one major idea for your postcard and make sure you explain that idea simply so that the reader can understand what you're offering and what they need to do.

Use a strong call to action. The *"call to action"* is what you want the reader to do.

- Do you want them to call a number and schedule a free estimate?

- Do you want them to call and purchase your product over the phone?

- Do you want them to enter a contest?

Your call to action should be powerful.

After all, this is the part where you want to get the potential customer to take advantage of your offer.

To help your call to action work, make sure the reward you're offering is good enough to get people to ACT.

The more effort that you require on the part of the potential customer, the greater the reward you need to offer. For example if you want the reader to go online and fill out a long form then you'd better be offering a great reward for their time and effort.

We suggest simple rewards for minimal effort. People just don't fill out long forms any more. Contact information is about all you're going to get nowadays.

Track your results. With any marketing campaign you want to track your results. Remember test and track.

Contrary to popular belief, the US mail is alive and well. It seems that a number of Internet marketers are finding that post cards work very well as another form of marketing. They are actually coming back into use very effectively.

You can see some great examples of direct marketing postcards by going to www.expresscopy.com. However I do not recommend that you use them for your printing needs as they are very expensive and their customer service has been very hit or miss.
However I do strongly recommend Vistaprint or Ps Print for all of your printing business needs; we have used both with outstanding results and their prices and turnaround times are excellent.

Telemarketing

Of course, this is calling people on the phone and trying to sell them a product or service. When most people hear the word "telemarketing" they cringe. It's horrible, right?

Then why do some people still use telemarketing? Because it works in some markets! (There is the high end market that Telemarketing is the norm, because it takes a Trader to sell a Trader.)

And it works best when the telemarketing follows a direct mail campaign. In fact, telemarketing has been shown to increase the effectiveness of direct mail marketing well over 100%!

Here is how you should follow-up direct mail marketing with telemarketing:

- Identify yourself and tell the person why you're calling.

- Tell them that you recently sent them a postcard and then give them a call to action.

- For example, you call and say, "Hi, this is Joe Smith from XYZ Company. I'm just giving you a quick call to follow-up on a postcard I sent you a few days ago. The postcard was for a 50%

discount on XYZ services. The offer will be running out at the end of the month and I wanted to give you a quick call to make sure you don't miss out on this opportunity.

So, when is a good time to set an appointment so you can take advantage of XYZ services today and save well over $XXX ?"

You can also use telemarketing to contact businesses in your area. To do this you just need a script – what you (or a representative for you) will say on the phone.

In the script all you need to do is say who you are and give the reason you're calling.

Ask to speak with the decision maker at the company. Get through this screen to the decision maker, and then repeat who you are and why you're calling the decision maker, and finally give a call to action.

So a basic script would be something like:

"Hello this is Joe Smith from XYZ Company. I'm calling to offer a great discount on XYZ. Who in the company handles XYZ purchasing? Rather than just leave my name and number, I'd rather arrange a better time when I can call back so I can speak with him/her. This offer ends in two days."

This should get you through the screener to the person who can actually decide to do business with you.

Then you can say to that person, "Hi this is Joe Smith from XYZ Company. I'm calling because I'm currently offering a great deal on XYZ. I'd like to personally come in and speak with you about it and give a brief demonstration. Would tomorrow morning be best for you?"

Boxes in businesses

Placing a box in a business can be great for your business. What you do is run a contest and you have people fill out a brief form with their name, address, and phone number. They drop the form into a box. Then you will have a box full of leads for your business.

There are a number of ways you can get someone to place a box in their business.

For example, if you're a window cleaner then you can offer to clean the business's Windows for free in exchange for them allowing you to put the box in their place.

Or maybe you can work out a 50% discount with a few different businesses. Then you'll have the extra business and you'll be capturing a lot of leads, too.

Trade programs are back (they never really left). This allows you to trade services or product for some other club member services or products.

Once you get all the leads, then you draw one winner for the contest. For everyone else, you get in touch with them and tell them who won the contest but then tell them they have won a consolation price and they'll get your services for 50% off or some other sales promotion that you are offering.

We know one restaurant that collects business cards in a bowl all month long and at the end of each month they draw out one card and that person gets one FREE pie of their choice.

All the other people get a 10% discount off their next visit.

Then they are on the e-mail mailing list and get weekly specials and belong to the pie of the month club. That means as a customer each time you go into the restaurant you can drop your card in the bowl and have another chance to win. There are a number of multiple winners of the pie of the month club; their pictures are placed in the store and on the store website, blog, and Facebook page.

How to tap into what's hot

Now we are going to take a look at five ways you can tap into what's hot at any given time in order to really boost your business.

Here are five strategies:

1. **Networking works.**   Networking is when you meet and create relationships with other people who might be able to help you and your business. On the surface, networking is pretty selfish and in the end it's a little selfish. But in order to network successfully you really need to help others out so that they'll be more willing to help you out. This is the old "you scratch my back and I will scratch yours", this is alive and well and works.

We have found that helping others (now mind you this does not mean that you are to give away the business) generally works and networking is no exception!

For example, you might call a radio station and offer to clean their Windows or carpets for free.

Or you might call a newspaper and offer to clean every window in their building for free. Why would you do such a thing?

Well, to start a relationship with them.

Maybe they'll wind up hiring you to always clean their Windows or maybe they won't. But more importantly, now you've got a foot in the door with powerful sources of media. There's no telling how much this is worth.

Maybe the newspaper highlights a local business every week and now they'll be more inclined to do a profile on you.

In our particular area the local paper profiles one small business per week.

Maybe one of the DJs at the radio station will mention that you cleaned the Windows and that you did a great job. Who knows?

That last one is a stretch, but you never know when a DJ might take a liking to you or your work.

But forming relationships with other businesses and people (networking with them) will help you and your business in ways you can't possibly imagine.

The effectiveness of word-of-mouth advertising is undeniable.

Another great place to network is at the local Chamber of Commerce. If you aren't already a member you need to become one right away. And you should always attend any business events that take place in your area.

Usually there are monthly meetings or events for local businesses. (Just make sure that you have your elevator pitch prepared before you go to such an event. This speech should be one of the first things that you do while making a business plan. You should use this right after you say "Hello").

There are other organizations that you can join too. These will help produce leads (potential customers) for you. LeTip International (www.letip.com) is one organization. BNI (www.bni.com) is another great organization.

Networking is the most powerful marketing tool you can use. So if you have a limited budget, always be on the lookout for new networking opportunities. (All of the Social Media can be used for networking now.)(This will be discussed more in upcoming chapter where we will look at targeting commercial and residential customers.)

2.   Use holidays and seasons to your advantage.   You can tie many of your marketing promotions into holidays and seasonal events that are taking place. At any time during the given year there's almost always something going on.

Here's a quick rundown of just a few of them (in the order that they happen):
New Year's Day, Martin Luther King Day, Valentine's Day, Presidents' Day, April fools, Easter, Earth Day, Mother's Day, Mori all day, Father's Day,

Fourth of July, summer specials, Labor Day, Fall, Columbus Day, Halloween, Thanksgiving, Chanukah, Christmas, and New Year's Day.

And this is just a sample of the major holidays. If you look at most calendars you'll see that just about any day has some kind of holiday attached to it.

As often as possible, tie into these events and holidays. Offer promotional materials that might go along with a certain time of the year or can run into another season.

For example, on the Fourth of July you might sponsor a float for the local parade.

Or maybe you'll pay to have your business logo and phone number printed on red, white, and blue Frisbees.
Then you can walk around the parade handing out Frisbees to kids.

Another example would be running an ad at the beginning of summer (or in the spring) that talks about enjoying the summer sunshine.

You could highlight how great it is to go have the summer sunshine streaming into your house. Then go into the importance of having clean windows that actually let the sunshine in. (Can't you hear the radio ad now? That song from the musical "Hair," "let the sun shine and," would be playing in the background.)

On the other hand you could be just a little contrary, and do something different. Hire a kiddie jumper on a summer day in your parking lot to bring parents and children to your show room/store.

In fact, go out right now and buy a giant 90-day planner at your local office supply store and map your marketing plans against the holidays and other events on the calendar.

3.   Grab onto fads.   There are a lot of other trends and fads you can tap into as well. You can look at what's making news and create a marketing promotion around that. Even if it doesn't relate to your specific service, you can still tie into it.

For example, for the last few years global warming has been a huge issue.

Almost everyone wants to do their part.
So, you could run an ad that you use products that are completely natural and eco-friendly.
You would tie into the movement for everyone to go green. This could be a big promotion around Earth Day.

You can make your store a free drop off for "hard to get rid of products".

4. Always look for the latest and greatest.   Always keep your eyes and ears open for the <u>latest and greatest invention in your business.</u>

If a product is created that revolutionizes the way carpets are cleaned then you want to be the first to get it.
If you are fast, you can advertise that you have technology that none of your competitors have.

Here is one of the places that mainstream media can be of help.
They can be one of the places to find a new fad. Look in your trade journals and magazines, and related fields.

5. Use movies and other forms of entertainment. Movies and other forms of entertainment – sporting events, award shows, concerts, Street fairs, etc. – always offer a great marketing opportunity. You can make a video of something that you have done as a promotion and post it on your web site.

Get several businesses that are close to you and have a week end sale, an evening sale. Make any excuse to have a gathering and get your customers involved.
People are always talking about these things.

If you can tap into them then you can really boost your business.

For example, if there is a huge event coming to your town, you should run an ad that mentions the need for everyone to get their home looking as nice as possible for all the people who will be coming into town.

Part of that would be getting their windows and or carpets cleaned.

All of the above ideas are great ways for marketing your business.

How to get free publicity (or nearly free)

There are many different ways that you can market your business. These go way beyond simply making sure everything you do is making you and your business look good. Almost all types of marketing will cost you money.

However, there are many marketing techniques that won't cost you a dime.

You've probably heard the saying: "there's no such thing as bad publicity."

Well, this isn't exactly true. There are more than a few companies – some of them huge companies – that were ruined just because they got bad publicity.

But most of the time publicity is a great thing. There are a few different ways that you can get publicity that's completely free (or nearly free).

Of course you want to make sure that all publicity you get is positive publicity. And the publicity you're after is through the media.

(Later in this report we'll go over how to write a press release so you can let the media know when you're doing something extraordinary.)

The first type of great publicity is donating to a charity.

Obviously this isn't free publicity but the media coverage you get is often worth much more than the amount of money you donate.
For example, you might donate $XXX to the local fire department so they can buy some new equipment.

The local newspaper and the local television station come out and cover it.

Now you're on the six o'clock and 11 o'clock news.

You're also in the paper.

Not only are people seeing you and your business but they're also seeing what a great person you are.

Pretty much everyone who sees this news story will see you as a good business for their neighborhood and if they need what you're selling they will be more inclined to use your business.

Establishing yourself as an expert is a great way to get free publicity, too.

You can write an article on how to properly care for your carpets. Include a couple tips that most people don't know and then see if your local newspaper will run it. If they do then you are an instant expert in your field.

You can capitalize on that.

You could take it to the next level and tell the paper that you will do a free weekly Q&A section on carpet cleaning and care of all types of floors.

The paper gives you a byline. This is where you put in your business name, your name, what your business does, and how to get in touch with you. This positions you as the Local Expert.

Not only will you get business from people who see your article but you'll also continue to get business because of how you can position yourself as an expert who had an article published in a local paper.

Another way to get publicity is to offer creative promotions.

The more creative a promotion is the better chance you'll have that the media will cover the promotion.

One example would be offering to clean the winner's house windows for free for a year if they win a contest. Of course this isn't very creative. There are certainly more creative contests that you can think of.

But one advantage to running a contest is that you can ask that everyone who enters the contest give you their mailing address and e-mail address.

This will allow you to build a list of names and addresses so that you can market directly to these people.

Obviously there are more ways to get publicity. However, these are three of the best ways.

You can't underestimate the power of publicity. Bad publicity will ruin your business but good publicity can turn your business and you into an overnight success story.

So the first rule of good publicity is to stay away from bad publicity.

And then make sure you create your own positive publicity.

Internet marketing.

Since the Internet became available in homes, people have been making money online.
The Internet has turned out to be an absolute Goldmine for thousands and thousands of people.
Obviously you're familiar with the Internet since you got this book there. So that's a good thing.
You already have a leg up on many small business owners.

However, there are probably a lot of things about the Internet that you don't know. These things can really help your business.
And you're about to discover exactly how the Internet can help you succeed.

First of all, if you don't have a website then you need to get one.
Your website can be a blog or just a straight up website. We favor Blogs

as they tend to get more repeat traffic and interact with your customer, and that is a big thing now.

A blog is to get more customers involvement than just a website. It is not just to sell your wares it is to communicate with your customers, as they expect more of that now.

First you have to get a domain name.

Even if you don't know much about computers, it won't take you very long to setup your own Domain name.

Have to get your Domain hosted, and then have a website or blog created for you.

Or you can create yourself. It gets easier every year/month as new applications are appearing faster and faster each week even.

Most sites that sell domain names are also hosting companies, I don't agree with the philosophy that some Internet marketers have buying their domains from one company and then hosting with another company they managed to save a few dollars per domain over time but I'm not sure whether it's worth the hassle or not.

One of my favorites is BlueHost (at least as we go to press) and Bills is HostGator is one of the better domain service companies. There are so many Hosting companies that we have only listed our main favorites. There's also a company out there called NameCheap (I also use them for some of my hosting and they do a real good job of taking care of my needs and problems any time that I have called them), they also offer inexpensive alternative for Internet marketers.

You want your domain name to reflect your USP/elevator pitch / Headline, if at all possible, <u>make sure your domain is name is also easy to understand or remember.</u>

For Best recognition and easy to remember is having a .com 2nd best would be an .org. Third-best would be a .net.

When it comes to setting up your personal site or blog if you feel comfortable enough to build it go for it. With Wordpress it is really simple and just takes some of your time to sit down and learn how to use it. There is some easy tutorials online where you can learn from Basic to Advanced at Specky boy design magazine.

If you don't feel comfortable doing it yourself, you can have a built for you and not cost you an arm & a leg. There is a number of places that you can go to get your site built. Craigs list, Fivver, or even in your local ads.

A cheaper alternative to having your own page or site set up on a social networking site. You've probably seen businesses that have MySpace pages or Facebook fan pages.

You can easily set your own page up.

Even if you don't know much about computers, it won't take you very long to setup your own page.

Not only will a presence on the Internet help you look more professional, but it will also land you new customers.

When you setup your pages you want to make sure your target keyword phrases that will help people find you.

So, if you run a window cleaning service in bedrock then you would want to target the keyword phrase "window cleaning service in Bedrock."

You would probably also want to target other keys word phrases like "need my Windows cleaned in Bedrock" and "window cleaning service in Bedrock."

What you are doing is making sure the search engine (like Google, Bing and yahoo) pull up your page when people type those keyword phrases into the search box.

So think of anything people might type as a search phrase to get "window cleaning services in Bedrock" then target those keywords.

You should target those keywords by making sure they are sprinkled throughout the text on your page. (Rule of thumb is no more than 3 times of each keyword in 500-600 total words.)

If you have your own website or blog then you want to make sure those keyword phrases are in the meta-tags.

Now, you can also take advantage of many different ways to advertise your business online. This is what Internet marketing is all about.
It's marketing online for the purpose of making money. You can pay to advertise on the Internet.
The huge search engine, Google, has a program that's called "Google Ad Words."
This allows you to advertise your business for certain keywords.
This is just like the keywords you would target for your own website.
They should be words that people will use when searching for your service in your area. Because the keywords won't be very popular (since they are specific to your area) this will help keep the costs down.
However, it will still cost you money. = Ad words. But they work.

You can also advertise on other local businesses sites. This will usually cost you money too unless you do a banner / ad exchange.
But you might be able to find another business in your area that compliments your business for this type of exchange.

There are a number of free Internet marketing techniques that you can use as well. These include article writing, blogging, social networking, pod casts, and creating videos.

There are article submission sites (for example, ezinearticles.com) where he you can submit short articles (about 300 – 500 words) and then have them posted on that site so other people can read them.
From these submission sites your article can and maybe post it to other sites throughout the Internet, it's kind of a bonus for posting your article in an open forum.
This will then create back links to your site and you as the writer of the post / article.

Having a business on the Internet offers more possibilities than any brick-and-mortar business can.
The more content you have on the Internet, the more likely you are to be found by potential customers.
The bigger content base that you can show, adds more credibility to your

business, especially on the Internet.
As we see it brick-and-mortar business is too limiting, by having an
Internet marketing business your choices are endless.

You should have two main goals with your Internet marketing:
to be found when people are searching for a business such as yours, and
to help potential customers with problems or questions.
Creating and posting content will help you accomplish both of these goals.

Let us show you how.

Why a blog?

Blog is short for "web log" and that's just what it is.
It is like an online Journal.
You can sign-up for a free blog at WordPress.com or at blogger.com; you
can even get your blog added as part of your main site.
Blogs take many different designs as far as a business marketing styles.
Your blog could be story style, like a story of your life what you do
throughout the day, (that is if you lead a somewhat abnormal life style) I
would believe that would be in its self a story of you or your business.
(Keep in mind here that the number of reality shows on TV. That is
becoming a HUGE market, so why couldn't yours be one? A mini reality
blog / story / whatever you want to call it.)
As a review site you find a product that you like and write a review about
it, if it has a large enough audience then it could be a site all of its own.
This type of site is generally considered an affiliate site; after you review
the product you generally have sales pages for the different products that
you review where you are making a commission on each sale.

Then you could have a story of how you acquired some merchandise that
you're selling or what you went through to be able to sell it.

Then there is the blog Carnival, a Carnival is just like a magazine except
that it's online. Certain bloggers host carnivals about one topic or another
and you can submit your blog post to be included.
If the hosting blogger agrees to feature your post, the Carnival will

introduce your contribution and include a link for your interested readers to read your post on your blog.

Turns out there is a great place to see all the carnivals taking place at submit your post to those whose topic relates to your content.
http://BlogCarnival.com/
I could probably go on for a couple of hours just on blog topics, but this book is all about promoting your business. We believe that blogging and now Facebook is vital to your Brand / USP / Elevator Pitch.

Your blog can include instructional videos for new products that you have on how to install and set up them.
Until your readers that you will have new videos coming out every week this way you'll get them come back to see what's next.
This helps create excitement for your business and your website/blog.

Each one of your main products can have its own blog or website, and you want these blogs to all point back to your main blog or business blog/website.
This is where you also have links out to your YouTube videos, your twitter site, your Facebook fan page, your LinkedIn home page and any other social media that you may belong to point back to your main blog. All of that helps your total ranking with all of the search engines.

There's a lot more that you can learn about Internet marketing.
But now you know the basics so you can either hire someone to set these things up for you or with a little time and effort you can easily set them up yourself.
There's one more important part of Internet marketing that you need to know and that is on each one of your sales pages, blogs, or website you need to have what is called an "opt in box".
This is the box that your potential customers can fill out (with their name and e-mail). You can offer them a small gift (a free report) or simply some information about your business in exchange for them giving you their information.
Once you have their information you can market to them through e-mail

marketing.

And that's what Internet marketing is all about, collecting their name so you can email them and keep them informed of what your business is doing (new products or services) and to market to them. Send mostly information that they might be interested in and a once a week / month advertisement that way when the ad comes it doesn't make them mad but they might actually look forward to getting your ads because you respect their time.

One of the tools you'll have to help you here is an auto responder. What that does is when your customers put in their name and e-mail addresses and submit them to your opt in box your auto responder begins sending out e-mails to that person that just joined your mailing list. That person begins to receive e-mails from you on a prescribed schedule that you choose. The e-mails, sales letters, content and more are written by you, to help you engage more with your customer. The best part about the auto responder is once you set it up, the auto responder will completely run on its own. All that you have to do is add a new e-mail letter each week or twice a week so that the customer gets accustom to seeing your tips and tricks that will help save him money around his business or home.

This is one of the best ways of effectively engaging your customers for practically no cost at all, just a little time.

To help networking and growing education in your field join some local groups like the Chamber of Commerce, Toastmasters, or if you live in the San Francisco Bay Area you could attend one our MeetUp groups in Livermore and Walnut Creek, California.

http://meetup.com/Webify-Business-Club-Tri-Valley

http://meetup.com/East Bay SEO/Internet Marketing Meetup
Check the site for days and times.

www.theNewMarketingBasics.com

8
SOCIAL MARKETING / MEDIA / NETWORKING

Social marketing is taking the nation by storm and is changing the way that businesses talk to their customers and market to their customers.
Social media provides the way that people can share ideas, thoughts, content and relationships online.
This differs from so-called "mainstream media" content where no one can comment on anything, ever, unless you write the publisher.
With Social Media anyone can create content and comment on it.

Social media can take the form of text, audio, video, images, and forums.

Social networking sites:
are a great place to promote your business.

There is a number different social networking sites that you can follow and use it as places to promote your business.
Here is a list of just the most popular, Facebook, MySpace, Squidoo, hub pages, LinkedIn, MeetUp and Twitter just to name a few.
If I didn't mention your favorite social site I am sorry, there are just too many to list all of them here.
Finally, people love to watch videos, and even the most basic videos are watched by others.
You can create a basic video and post it to YouTube, after you have

created your account. All you need is a Webcam and/or some free video making software.

Here's a short list of free video making software:

Microsoft Movie Maker, this is one that already comes installed on your Windows computer.

This movie maker has drag-and-drop features to make creating and editing your movies easier.

Microsoft has many add-ons for this software, and the upgrades are available through the website.

This is just one of the best free video editing software programs available.

Apple iMovie, this is comparable to Windows movie maker, but Apple iMovie is used on the Mac operating system.

This has many advanced features and add-ons. Unfortunately, the software is only free if you buy a new Mac system, if you want the software without buying the system, it is available for purchase. The best free video editing programs available for Mac users from Apple.

Avid Free DV, this software is available for both Windows and Mac operating systems, and includes basic video and audio editing capabilities, as well as up to two streams of real – time effects.

On the whole, a solid video editing program that is slightly hard to use, but very powerful when you learned its ins and outs.

Wax, is a high-performance flexible free video editing software program. It started out as a college student project, and has sense grown.

This program is good for both home users and professionals. It can be used as a stand – alone application, or as a plugin to other video editors. The software also features unlimited video and audio tracks with top – down composing.

Facebook fan pages or groups?

Best description I've seen is "groups are great for organizing on a personal level and for smaller scale interaction around a cause.

Pages are better for brands, businesses, bands, movies, or celebrities who want to interact with their fans for customers without having them, connected to a personal account, and we have a need to exceed Facebook's 5000 friends' cap".

As a fellow business owner, you already know that marketing is important for business growth and in today's climate that's especially true. Facebook is a great tool for this purpose.

More and more, your prospects are turning to social networking websites like Facebook to locate businesses in their own backyard, or to ask their "Facebook Friends" for product and service recommendations.

Facebook is getting more than 132 million unique visitors per month and their traffic has grown by more than 45% in the last year alone. (2009 to 2010)

According to Facebook's statistics, they have reached over 800 million active users.
·   50% of our active users log on to Facebook in any given day
·   Average user has 130 friends
·   People spend over 700 billion minutes per month on Facebook

When it comes to activity, Facebook users are prolific:

·   There are over 900 million objects that people interact with (pages, groups, events and community pages) Yours should be one of them.
·   Average user is connected to 80 community pages, groups and events
·   Average user creates 90 pieces of content each month
·   More than 30 billion pieces of content (web links, news stories, blog posts, notes, photo albums, etc.) are shared each month

With statistics like this, you should now understand why "Facebook is a BIG deal."

So, you might be wondering if your local business can really benefit from Facebook fanpages and the resounding answer is YES!

It's for this reason that we wrote "How Facebook Fanpages Can Generate More Profits" to give you a clear understanding of what "Facebook Fanpages" are used for and why Facebook is something you should care about.

According to the Facebook Pages Manual, Facebook decided to add the functionality of setting up fanpages so that business owners, organizations, bands, and celebrities could keep a close relationship with their fans, clients, and customers.

Having a Facebook Fanpage gives you the capability of adding video, graphics, and email auto responders to start building a list, adding coupons, selling gift cards, etc.
You can be very creative with Facebook fanpages, just like you can with your website. So you might be thinking "So what is the big deal, I do all those things on my website already." Although you might have all of these things on your website already, getting your business more exposure on the world's largest Social Network should also be part of your marketing strategy.

There is a sample Fanpage that is selling gift cards on our website, along with a sample of a Fanpage that has an email auto responder on it so that they can collect emails and start building a profitable list.
There are also ways to feature products that your business sells:
Overall, there are a number of creative ways for you to use a Facebook Fanpage for your business, and that is why we at," The New Marketing Basics", wants to help you with your Facebook Fanpage, if you need help.

Do Fanpages get picked up in the Search Engines?   YES, quickly!

Well, when you get a Fanpage, you are going to need to know how to promote your Fanpage right?
There are a number of ways your Fanpage can get visitors, and surprisingly the easiest way is by getting your Fanpage recognized by the search engines.

Facebook Fanpages are getting Search Engine indexing and ranking and therefore they are bringing organic traffic to your page.

When it comes to Facebook Fanpages, the keyword that we want to focus on is "Business owners." When a business owner has the capability to promote their product or service, a tightly focused keyword rich Fanpage will get ranking in the search engines.

For us, the key word here is "businesses" because when we use a Fanpage for a niche specific keyword/product that is our business.

With a tightly keyword-focused Fan Page, you will be indexed fast by the search engines. Your individual fan page will let you be recognized as an expert in your niche with exposure to potentially thousands of people each day, build your list, generate traffic to your blogs or websites, and much, much more.

Facebook has taken over Google as the website with the most traffic. Imagine having a Fanpage that can be in front of that many people? How would you like a piece of that action? You Can!

Another great reason for marketing with Facebook Fanpages is that there are so many different ways to use this website to market your websites and products and many ways to turn your visitors and fans into buying machines.

With the ability to easily share videos, pictures, status updates, and many other bits of information with all your Facebook fans, you can easily stay in front of people in this social networking community.

So How Else Do I Promote my Fanpage?   There are a few ways that you can promote your Fanpage. Using the Facebook advertising platform is the best way to promote your business. We will cover how the paid advertising platform can get you traffic and we will also give you other FREE ideas you can use to get traffic to your Fanpage.

Let's begin with Facebook Pay Per Click….   You've seen them yourself, most likely…those ads running down the right-hand side of your Facebook pages, most of them about interests you particularly enjoy.

You are not seeing the same ads as everyone else accessing Facebook at that moment. These ads are specifically targeted to data Facebook has gleaned from your preferences and other sources.

Facebook ads are simple but powerful. Each one consists of a title, text block and graphic or photo of your choice—all within an 110px X 80px "box", to fit that vertical, right hand Facebook sidebar.

If you think of them as a cross between a Twitter tweet and a banner ad, you've just about got the picture!

And yes—they absolutely can advertise your:

· Product
· Services
· Contest
· Cause
· Links
· Photos
· Videos
· Unique Selling Proposition (USP)
· Business Event

Facebook's biggest benefit is its most obvious.

It operates through social networking and trending rather than pure SEO—the hottest trend of this brand new decade.

It allows readers to see your ads on their mobile phones—and mobile devices now outnumber personal computers, 4 to 1!

Did you catch that? Cell phones outnumber PCs by 4 to 1!

WOW! That was quick. *See Chapter 9*

If you are using Facebook Advertising to promote your Fanpage, you will find that the traffic you are buying is much cheaper than Google Adwords.

Adwords can be dangerous if you do not know what you are doing; Facebook advertising for your Fanpage can be a great first start if you are new to Pay Per Click marketing.

But whether you use Adwords (SEO-based) or Facebook ads (social networking-based), Facebook ads nowadays are a "must"— particularly with the not-so-subtle switch-over to mobile devices!
But it's great for beginning marketers because—at the moment—it's significantly less expensive to advertise on Facebook than with PPC on Google!

Graphics Capability— Facebook's other big benefit is that you can introduce a graphic element or photo into what is basically just a small text ad!
Since Facebook is "tuned" to graphic elements, and interest has been shown to peak when graphics are displayed, it wins hands-down over Adwords banner ads.

Text Capability— You have 75 words to say what you want to say in Google Adwords (that's less than half a tweet!) Facebook ads not only allow you a 25-character headline, but 135 words of body text, too. (That's over double Google Adwords' capacity—but note that spaces count as always.)

What Businesses are Currently Using Fanpages?

Some people will tell you that Facebook Ads don't work for business purposes, but that's simply not so.
It should speak volumes and give you a big, fat clue about its potential when you realize that major companies are taking full advantage of Facebook Ads, in creative ways.

For example, according to Facebook's own Marketing Solutions page,

- Honda recently used Facebook Ads to keep consumers updated (and do serious damage control) after its recent spate of shocking recalls.

- Budweiser encouraged social interactivity with its customers when it invited them to select which commercials to show during televised sports games.

- Guitar Hero became the first online video game to reach 1,000,000 fans on Facebook

Even Coca-Cola jumped on the bandwagon, selling "virtual bottles of coke" and promising to donate $1.00 for every virtual bottle sent to their favorite cause.

These 4 examples (above) alone show you the sort of creativity you can employ (and flexibility you can take advantage of) when you mix a Facebook Fanpage and a Facebook Advertising campaign!

This company used a custom "Fanpage" to collect emails:
the Toyota Company.

If you already have a Fanpage for your business, you'll notice that this one has a number of features not found in the default layout.

Facebook allows businesses to customize their fanpages in a number of ways and doing so is a great idea!

You can add custom graphics to build your brand, videos that excite your visitors and deliver your message in a fresh, new way or even add the ability to capture email leads direct from your Fanpage!

You Want to Attract "Fansumers"

If you've been wondering what a "Fansumer" is, it's yet another social phenomenon you can use to your advantage.
According to Forrester Research, a "Fansumer" is simply a consumer who has "become a fan" of a brand on Facebook, this could be your brand.

This brings us back to yet another of Facebook Ads' biggest advantages... interactivity.

It's a proven maxim: Get people to engage as a participant, rather than as a spectator, and their stake in what they're engaging in becomes personal and more positive.

Use an app or a product and click the little "become a fan" text link on your Facebook page, and you are not only contributing to its statistical popularity, but you are personally endorsing it!

Why Profile Pages Can Be Your Best Friend.

The main reason you can target so specifically, in spite of Facebook itself having a broad, generic demographic, can be attributed to profile pages.

Think about it,
When you filled out your profile page, you were prompted to share your:

· Hobbies and interests
· Career and work information
· School, college or university
· Tastes in music, books and movies
· Personal and contact information (date of birth, marital status, etc.)
· City and state

And as much extra information as you chose to share. Among the things you share you can bet people can find great long-tailed keywords! These are what you should use when creating your Facebook Ads— targeted specifically to your ideal customer, of course.

Use your keyword in your headline at the very least—and again in the text (always providing it feels totally natural:
Remember, Facebook puts "social" before "SEO").

Other Ways to Drive Traffic to Your Fanpage

Even the most attractive fanpages are useless without visitors and that's why we utilize many different traffic-generation strategies on behalf of our clients.

We do our best to help you dominate the search engine results in an effort to bring you targeted traffic that is meaningful to your business.

Just a few of these strategies include...

· Search Engine Optimization (both on-page and off)
· Article Marketing
· Press Releases
· Blogging/RSS Feed Syndication
· Social Bookmarking
· Utilizing "Web 2.0" properties (like Facebook.com, Twitter.com etc.)
· Video Marketing (like YouTube.com, Viddler.com, etc.)
· Online Classifieds (like Craigslist.org, Kijiji.com, Patch.com, etc.)
· And a whole lot more!

Whether you are looking to make direct sales from your Fanpage, build leads or encourage your visitors to stop by your store or office, we can develop a traffic-generation strategy to meet your objectives.

Where Do We Go From Here?

If you're ready to build a solid online social networking presence and attract new fans to your Fanpage resulting in more business, we'd love to discuss your individual needs.

We offer the setup of Facebook fanpages, Facebook advertising and many other services for your business.

LinkedIn

Is another Social site which for the most part is used by business for business or what is called B2B (business to business) sales.
According to LinkedIn, it is a venue to help you locate that dream job; they have a whole section devoted to the job seekers.
A couple of tips for you jobseekers:
to ensure your profile is complete and up-to-date, your connections should represent your "real world" network.

This is true for business owners also.

Your LinkedIn profile is the first thing you do when you join LinkedIn, but just putting up any profile isn't enough.

It's important to make your profile relevant and compelling. It may need some editing.

You can check your profile numbers who visit you on the right side of your page.

If it reads, "15 people visited your profile this week" your profile is probably OK, but, if it reads 0 (zero) then some changes are in order.

Here are some reasons your LinkedIn profile may not be getting enough visitors:

1.   You don't make enough requests for people to join your network. Anytime you social media marketing you need to be consistent in your participation.

2.   You don't get many questions in your LinkedIn inbox each week. Answering these questions allows others to like you, respect your information, eventually trust you and ultimately make a purchase from you.

3.   You don't join as many groups related to your business as you can handle.

These to be possible clients or customers, or groups of like businesses that help one another and learn the ways of LinkedIn.

4.   You don't comment and add useful information to various groups (I recommend groups with growing numbers of active members).

To help you choose a group that you are considering joining, check under the "member's link" to see what people are doing and what they're talking about.

This should help give you a better picture of what this group is about.

5.   You don't have strong recommendations from clients.

These really matter, so ask for a recommendation and make it easy for them to give you a recommendation.

Present a sample of benefits or phrases to shortcut the time your past customers will have to spend, because they are helping you a lot make it easier for them.

If you're feeling like you're not getting enough of targeted visitors to your site or the numbers aren't growing fast enough, then you need to think of more ways to monetize your LinkedIn site.

How to monetize your LinkedIn experience and profile:

1. Make your first name/title in your profile one that shares what you do for your customers. That means added benefit after your name. For example, "your name" helps business people brand their company with the book. Always think from your visitor's point of view. What do they want? Why would they want to connect with you?

2. Provide in your profile only the details that showcase yourself, your business, and that support your purpose. This is more about your elevator pitch and USP.

3. Know the purpose for being in LinkedIn. My purpose was to connect with my primary best audience – business people, coaches, consultants, speakers and leaders who want to become more visible and credible. And this audience wants to get the number one credibility for their business by writing a book for their audience wants and needs.

4. Target your profile summary to your audience.
Notice your sentences that begin with "I". Don't over use the word "I". Instead, give some benefits of what your business can do for your clients or customers.
Right from the, "YOU", point of view. It's far more engaging.
Even ask a few questions about where your audience is now with their problem or challenge, that you can help solve. Think of your USP / Elevator Pitch.

5. You need to educate in your profile copy. Those that educate your customer find that it is the best way to market yourself.

Don't start your sentence with "I"; rather put "YOU" in your copy. What can you do for your visitors of your profile? For example, "you will get these benefits…"

6. Change your specialties a little on your profile page. Instead of a lecture, just share a sentence such as, "I work with clients who want to gain much higher visibility and credibility in their business."

If you have room, add some details. For example, write strong, natural promotional copy for your business.

7. Gather some powerful testimonials from former clients. Post them under the "recommendations" heading off on your profile page. Add a few early on, and keep adding each month or so.

Is it worth spending time writing and editing your profile? Yes, because you want to make your best first impression on your LinkedIn audience. I also advise getting feedback from a writer/marketing professional who knows LinkedIn well.

When I do make a new connection, I always visit the person's profile to see if he or she is in my target audience, the ones whose likes and wants are in my demographics will be one that I will contact.

As a footnote it wouldn't hurt to make a positive comment and welcome visitors to your LinkedIn page.

Twitter

There is a guy on the Internet that swears you can master Twitter in 10 min. or less, now personally it took me longer than 10 min. just to read his manual. It was 19 pages long; I still think he is wrong.
Anyway, I don't want to scare you off but it will take you more than 10 min. to master Twitter. Not saying you have to master Twitter, but twitter is part of the online business experience and you will want to use it.

To some it is a nuisance, to others it's a godsend, what you do with it, and how you use it can make all the difference in the world. For what I see it can be a gold mine if used properly.

Now this is not meant to be a slap, that as I see it, twitter is like a three-year-old that is just learn that she/he can ask questions, "what you doing?" Welcome to Twitter.
So let's start by setting up your twitter account, this is where you pick your screen name and pick your time zone and list a blog if you have one, the location where you live at.

And here is where you get to create your one line bio, and also you have the opportunity to protect some of your information as well.
This is a good idea; always protect your personal information.
This is a good time for you to add additional devices for twittering from your smart phone.
During the setup process you will be setting up your notification preferences, you'll upload your profile picture, customize the look of your home page and change your password.

Next you're going to be announcing yourself! Now you start playing follow the leader, the people you know and start following them always invite them to follow you too. Look for people to follow in the public timeline if you want.
At some point in time it's going to be necessary for you to flip this coin so to speak, that means you're going to have to start getting more followers, because that's how you're going to make money.

Finding the followers is the big trick, start by promoting or tweeting your RSS data feeds. You need to have active followers that are interested in your niche. Sometimes having your data feeds published via the public timeline isn't enough.
This is where the tools that are out there can help you find followers, do use them they will make this process much easier. Most of them are pretty inexpensive and are huge time savers.

Another tip on how to find followers is based on keywords. Twilert is a great little web service that does just this; it is a Twitter application that let you receive regular e-mail updates of tweets containing your brand, product, service, and any other keywords that you really like.
Then there are products like "The Tweet Tank "which is a little script that runs on your computer and makes getting followers automatic.

There are applications out there to integrate MySpace, Facebook and twitter; these can be a big win for Mr. Retailer if he is able to put it to work for himself.

Bonus Tip:

Check with your employees to see if one of them might be willing to work your twitter account. How you compensate them for this is up to you. I have heard of some retailers are able to get that service fairly inexpensive compared to having a pro do the work, by using a current employee. DON'T ask them to do it for free ask them how much would they expect to get paid. Negotiate the cost, but be fair, this one activity can add dollars to your bottom line and be a bonus customer service rep as quick response.

Make sure that you link your twitter and your web site or blog to your other social media whatever you use. This is a personal Link Wheel. This is where all of your comments point back to your sales page where ever it is (Your blog / website or it could be on any of the social sites). Your sales pages can be in a number of locations and it can be a number of different products or services.

Now that you have a twitter account, what do you do with it?
My suggestions are:
Offer your customers a 10% discount on their next sale if they follow you and another 10% on one purchase each month that they keep following you. That way you keep them subscribed, but don't flood their account with a ton of posts.

OK, now your customers are following you, now get creative and start promoting your business or service to your twitter followers and see how fast they respond.

A good example of an offer, offer the next 5 customers that mention your tweet 50% (now the percentage that you offer is up to you) off of 1 item. You can do something every day or every week all depends on what you want to do and how much that your customers will put up with.

You might send tweets out 2 or 3 times per week that way you aren't bugging them. Make the offer worthwhile for them to want to act on it or it could bomb.

The number of variants that you can use on this type of offers is HUGE. Imagine.

Another tip would be to get your customers to retweet (RT) your ad and give them a discount for re-tweeting your offer. Now, they have to show you on their phone where they did the RT, this is only fair. They just can't say that they did it and expect the discount.

This is just a couple of tips about what you can do with twitter, there is many more check out our website.

You will find more at www.thenewmarketingbasics.com.

YouTube

By now I hope you know what YouTube is. YouTube is an online public communication site where video sharing is changing American culture and business.

The best explanation I've heard so far is young lady on YouTube; follow the link if it is still up.

http://www.youtube.com/watch?v=d2PbdIzAVKs

YouTube is a place where you could share the best card trick ever, or you can share a story, a song, a dance, or playing your favorite musical instrument.

You can share a statement about a candidate you like or dislike, or you can rant about something you care deeply about.

By the way did I tell you? You can demonstrate your product, show your product in action, and show exactly what it can do for you or your customer.

First thing you do is create yourself an account with YouTube, that's really easy to do on the create account page.

Make sure you leave checked "let others find my channel on YouTube if they have my e-mail address"; otherwise nobody will be able to find your YouTube videos.

Create an account and you're free to upload your videos to YouTube.

Before you upload videos to YouTube, be sure that you research your keywords that you want to use as "tags" on your video.

"Tags" are used to best describe the video, and they need to be keyword rich.

This is a part that it might be good to brainstorm with one of your friends about the keywords.

The one big thing you'll have going for you is most of the Amateur Videos are not even trying to get top rankings for keywords, they don't even think about it.

Keywords: well we are talking about keywords again, this like all the other sections talking about keywords they're very important part of your business. You can also use your USP / Elevator Pitch here.

Bonus TIP:

RELEVANCE of KEYWORDS:

When you're searching your keywords be sure you keep this in mind that the relevance of keywords matter also.

Not only exact word matches. (Relevance = Relating to the matter in hand) You would be surprised how well that works.

The big question is always what kind of videos get attention, generate buzz, and said a steady flow of traffic to your website? Well here you go with the six top video types.

6 characteristics of popular and profitable videos.

1. Funny -   funny is the word that is consistently typed in a phrase in the search engines on the Internet.
People love to laugh so you know this type of video is going to be a winner.

2. Weird -   let's face it, the Internet can be a weird place, with weird people, who like to create different media and enjoys being different at the same time. Weirdness may help your video get noticed if you don't mind being weird, then go for it

3 Inspiring   -   anything inspiring can become extremely popular, extremely fast. In example was the interview with God presentation (you may have heard about it... If not, look it up on Google). It was a huge Internet hit. Now there are several interviews.

4. Shocking   -   shocking videos may get a viral effect and even news coverage from both online and off-line news sources.
Especially with video because it is basically proof that the shocking thing is real.

5. Interesting -   any time you can peek the curiosity of your viewer and make them want to learn more about your product or service, it is a good thing.
Creating a curiosity may be especially useful considering that users who find your video on YouTube will actually have to take the effort to type in the URL and visit the site you are promoting.

6. Sexy   -   I shouldn't even really have to mention this one. Sex is always popular, and I cannot think of any instance when being described as sexy as ever been in a hindrance to selling a product. There is, however, here you must be very careful about the kinds of things you post about sexy, you don't want them taken wrong.

I When in doubt, leave Sexy out and save yourself the hassle.

Google +

Well by now you should have heard something about Google +, Circles, Sparks, Stream, and let us not forget +1's. Then you can even do video chat in the Hangouts with up to 10 people.

I think Google really has something here. Here is a quick look at the project that they put together.

Sharing is a huge part of the web, a part that we think could be a lot simpler. That's why they have been working on adding a few new things to Google: to make connecting with people on the web more like connecting with them in the real world. They hope you like what they've cooked up so far. And stay tuned, because there's more to come. Well that is what Google had to say about their latest project Google plus, I tend to believe them.

This is what Google has to say about circles. You share different things with different people. But sharing the right stuff with the right people shouldn't be a hassle. Circles makes it easy to put your friends from Saturday night in one circle, your parents or another, and your boss in a circle by himself, just like real life.

Now let's see what Google has to say about Sparks: "remember when your grandpa used to cut articles of the paper and send them to you? That was nice. That's kind of what Sparks does: look for videos and articles and it thinks you'll like, so when you're free, there's always something to watch, read, and share." Grandpa would approve. Well I'm a grandpa and I approve this message.

Now Google hangouts: bumping into friends while you're out and about is one of the best parts of going out and about. With hangouts, the unplanned meet-up comes to the web for the first time. Let buddies know you're hanging out and see who drops by for face to face to face chat. Until we perfect teleportation, it's next best thing.

Well let me tell you about **Google mobile instant upload**, taking photos is fun, sharing of photos is fun, getting the photos off your phone and onto the web is pretty much the opposite of fun. That's why they created instant upload: so that from now on, your photos upload themselves. You don't even have to say 'cheese'.

Now this thing called **huddle**, what they're saying here is texting is great, but not when you're trying to get six different people to decide on a movie. Huddle takes care of it by turning all those different conversations into one simple group chat, so everyone gets on the same page long before the thumb get sore.

For more about Google + and all that they have going there be sure to follow us back on our membership site.
Remember that you get a free 1 year membership when you buy this book.**

www.theNewMarketingBasics.com

9

MOBILE MARKETING

Now is the time to start

It hasn't been that many years ago when it wasn't even possible to browse the Internet with your mobile phone well today it is. You might think what's the big deal, but let me tell you it's a big deal. And the reason I say that is real simple I have children that are in their 30s and 40s and this is how they shop.

They don't use the Yellow Pages they don't go home and look it up on the Internet, they pick up their phone and start browsing the web and generally have their answer in a matter of less than a minute or two. Now that is instant gratification.

Don't ask a question with them around as one of them will pick up their phone and just Google the question to find you an answer.

Now you can do like a lot of other people have done with Internet marketing, leave it behind not do anything or do just the minimal requirements and that is just put up a website like I know a number of businesses have, and they think that gives them the Internet presence. That's kind of true but not totally true, having a webpage or site does not constitute doing business on the Internet.

If all you have is your address, with a map of course, your phone number and your hours that really is not much of a website that's more like a yellow page. That would be something that you would have for a mobile site.

So according to Nielsen media research, around 27% of mobile users have a smart phone. By the end of quarter of three 2011 that number is expected to almost double to around 50% of all mobile phone users. (Currently there are 63 Million smart phones in the US alone). The technology is getting better, and cheaper, making it easier for more people to have smart phones. It is amazing to think about, but the mobile web is growing four times as fast as the Internet.

So what does this mean for you? Depends on whether you want to be one of the early adopters are you want to come up behind and be one of the last ones to adopt this technology. The top companies in the world already have mobile sites because their research indicates that it is an important market to reach.

We bought software at the beginning of this year to create our QR codes. For those of you who don't know what QR code is, it is a specific matrix barcode (or two-dimensional code), readable by dedicated QR barcode readers and camera phones. The code consists of black modules arranged in a square pattern on a white background. The information encoded can be text, URL or other data.

When choosing your domain name for your mobile site, what domain might come to mind? That's right (your web site). MOBI. That's because it's became the standard companies used to develop mobile presence. You can go to http://mobile/.com/ to get additional help from the Mobi people.

Another way you might wish to do this is use a subdomain on the domain that you already have. You could do that too! You could set it up as the mobile.youraddress.com, m.youraddress.com, or yoursite.com/mobile. So as you see there's a number of ways you can do it. (Consult your webmaster.)

Always consider what would be best, and easiest, for your site visitors to remember and use, I would think that would be important. You can always use a link to your mobile site on your front / landing page.

Features your mobile website should have.

Visitors should be able to find what they're looking for without a lot of hassle. That means your site should be user-friendly. Unfortunately, most standard websites are designed to be viewed on a desktop or a laptop. So when people are viewing on it on their mobile screens, it doesn't quite look right. First thing is people have to scroll too much, things don't load properly or not at all, and it's a frustrating experience pretty much all the way around. Pictures and videos don't do well on a mobile unless they are optimized for mobile. (See your webmaster for help.)

Important to keep in mind that many people have limited data plans. So if your site sucks up a lot of bandwidth, chances are good that people are going to have a hard time viewing it or won't view it. Something else to think about is why are people are browsing your site. Is it because they're stuck somewhere and they are just killing time? Is it because they can't possibly wait until they get home to their computer and see what you have to offer? Or are they just trying to find some information quickly?

Considering these questions your customers have when viewing your mobile website they don't want a huge document to look through, so simple and concise is the way to go.

This also means that you need to be conscious about the different devices that are out there, it's not just the iPhone's, it's the blackberry, or the android. That means testing it out on different devices is probably a good idea, if not essential.

If you use one of the services that will talk about later, they take steps to ensure that it will be compatible. You can even test to see how it will look at all different devices using a viewer for that device.

W3.org (World Wide Web Consortium) specifies the requirements you should consider when designing your mobile site. They call this the default delivery context.

Delivery Default Context

Usable Screen Width	120 pixels, minimum
Markup Language Support	XHTML basic 1.1 delivered with content type application/XHTML plus XML
character encoding	UTF-8
Image format support	JPEG, GIF 89a
Maximum Total Page Weight	20 kilobytes
colors	256 colors, minimum
styles sheet support	CSS level I. In addition, CSS level II @ media rule together with the handheld and all media types.
HT TP	HTTP/1.0 or more recent HTTP 1.1
script	no support for client-side scripting.

This is adapted from http://www.w3.org/TR/mobile-bp/. You can visit this site to learn more about W3 best practices for mobile web. (consult with your webmaster if you don't understand this.)

W3 also discusses five particular areas we should pay attention to when formatting for the mobile web.
1. Overall Behavior
2. Navigation and Links
3. Page Layout and Content
4. Page Definition
5. User Input

Overall Behavior   Content should be accessible on all mobile devices. You can have content formatted to take advantage of a specific device, when it is appropriate. It's a good idea to test this out on emulators of the devices and, if possible, on the device itself.

Navigation and Links   Keep in mind that it can be tough for your users to type in the long and complicated web address. So you want to make it easy for them. For example, you can have your site automatically revert them to a mobile site when landing on your page with the mobile device. You can also buy a .Mobi address as your main address.

You have to think about their experience navigating around your site when they are already on your page. Try not to have complicated navigation at the top. Make it is basic, yet functional, as possible.

At the same time, you want to have enough links that they can easily find what they're looking for. Having a way for them to jump back to the top of the page is a great service − − especially if they've had to scroll down for a while!

Page layout and content, page definition, and user input.

W3 says, "Users in a mobile context are often looking for specific pieces of information, rather than browsing."
They recommend writing with the most prevalent information in the beginning so that people can tell whether the content is of interest to them. This should be what you are doing as good writing practices. (As a writer, you're used to having to capture people's attention right away! Key words with action words always work to help grab attention.)

Here are some key points to think about as far as layout, page definition, and user input goes as well:

Pay attention to this size of the page.
Ensure people do not have to scroll in more than one direction to read all of your content.
Keep navigation clean and simple.
Ensure graphics are kept to a minimum and really add to the experience.
Pay attention to the colors you use. They may not all be compatible with

all devices.
Page title should be short yet descriptive.
Do not use frames.
Use headings and subheadings.
Avoid tables.
Provide text for non-text items
validate your code using http://validator.w3.org/mobile/.
Minimal user input (i.e. forms to fill out).

Right about now, you might be excited about the challenge of creating your own mobile site. Or, if you're like many other people, you're absolutely terrified at the technical aspects. Thankfully, there are some services and tools available that will be a big help.

Once again, visit http://www.w3.org/TR/mobile-bp/ for more information about these practices. (This is really a techie place, so see your webmaster for help.)

Services that can help you create a mobile version of your site.

There are some great services you can use it practically do all the work for you! These sites have different features and benefits, so you need to find the one that is right for your site and your customers.

Site.MOBI   This is a great, and free, way to build your mobile site. Site.MOBI is a great one to go with if you consider yourself to be technically challenged. You don't have to download any software or use anything at all complicated. Best of all, the site you develop through site.MOBI can be viewed on any mobile phone. It's a great thing!

Another great feature is that you can host your mobile site wherever you would like to. This is something other free providers are missing, since they often require you to post on their network, unless you paid not to.

Other features include:

FORMS
AUDIO
VIDEO
MOBILE COMMERCE
MOBILE ads
Note that this service is hooked to Moby site galore, which is discussed below.

Find it at HTTP://site.MOBI.

Mippin   This is an interesting service in its also free! This probably isn't the service you want to go with if you want to become legally professional and hands on, but it's a great, nearly instant, way to get a mobile site that's perfect for many uses.

There is a small level of customization as far as layout and colors, so you will be able to express your style somewhat. Another bonus is that you can enter tags to make your site searchable with in Mippin.com. Keep in mind that your mobile site will have an address attached to Mippin, such as http://mippin.com/yourmobilesite.

Play around with Mippin – – you just might like it and it's definitely cost-effective since it's free!

Visit HTTP://www.mippin.com/web/.

Wirenode   Wirenode is another, free, service to create your mobile site with. It's easy to use as well. What's nice about this one is that you can try out the free version. Then, if you decide that Wirenode is right for you, you can upgrade to take advantage of even more features, such as having a custom URL (this is a great thing for most businesses).

You can consider the service to be somewhere between myth and in both foods as far as customization is concerned. You can choose your domain name, upload pictures, and track your site statistics. You can further customize how he your site looks, which is best for those who like to take a more hands-on approach.

Visit http://Www.wirenode.com/.

Zinadoo Zinadoo is yet another free tool. What's great about this one is that not only do you get a nice looking site, but there are integrated promotional tools. There are mobile and web widgets, text and e-mail services, optimization for Google mobile (through the use of tags), submission to the online business directory Zinadoo maintains, and access to Mobiseer.

Visit http://www.zinadoo.com/

Winkisiteyou guessed it – – this is another free service! Winksite is great because it's totally compliant with the standards W3C has set. It's also a nice way to integrate you into the mobile site building community. This solution will not be right for everyone, but it has a nice Web 2.0 feel to it.

Visit http://winksite.com.

Higher-end mobile sites

The services above will be just fine for many people. However, you might want to look into some more advanced options if you are serious about making your mobile site the best it can be. You'll get more customization and features, which is important for many businesses.

Mofuse Mofuse touts themselves as the "easiest way to be mobile." As you're aware, the mobile experience is different depending on which device you are using. Mofuse allows you to optimize for 5000 different mobile devices.

They also make it so you don't need to have a lot of "techie" knowledge to make it work. This is more cost effective because you can make any of the needed changes yourself.

If you'd like, Mofuse even offers to build the mobile site for you! This is a great way to save time, if you're willing to outsource its creation to make sure it's done right.

Mofuse helps you to promote your site, gives you a custom domain, gives you access to analytics, allows you to integrate your logo, and it has an easy to use content editor. This is a must for those who were not as experienced with web design. You can add content via RSS feed or through their content editor. This gives you more flexibility than others offer.

There are plans for starting at around $8 Per month going all the way up to $200 per month. This can be very cost-effective no matter which way you slice it! Find out more about the plans and what Mofuse has to offer by visiting:

http://mofuse.com/plans/.

2ergo   you can try the 2ergo services for more customization. This is part of the big leagues – – they've done the mobile site for the National Guard! Now, there is a Mobile Site Builder, but many choose to have2ergo customize their site.

These sites are nothing short of fantastic. They will detect a person's mobile device and carrier. *They allow for data capture, they integrate ads, have real time tracing, and have technical support available so you're never left hanging.*

You will need to contact 2ergo for a quote.

Visit http://www.2ergo.com

MobiSiteGalore   MobiSiteGalore has one many, many awards! In fact, many people choose them because they know they are going to end up with something great. They have a Website Builder, Quick Start Wizard, the ability to add pages and the color scheme, and more. They even allow you to check to ensure your site to meet mobile site standard.

Other things you can add to your site include add to phone book, click to call, Google search, and more. There are different price points, depending on your needs.

Visit http://www.mobisitegalore.com.

Creating a mobile version of your WordPress site.

WordPress has become a very powerful way to run your websites these days. It was designed as blogging software, but it can be customized to look like a standard website as well. Perhaps you're already taking advantage of the WordPress platform. If so, then you're well aware that there is a plug-in for just about anything you could possibly need for your site! That holds true for mobile as well. There is a plug-in that can easily render your site perfect for mobile devices.

MobilePress   this is a highly rated plug-in. It will automatically render your content to make it suitable for mobile devices. It comes out with some great features, including the ability to track your ads.

You'll be able to display ads from Admob, Quattro Wireless, Buzzcity, and imMobi (this information is straight from the http://wordpress.org/extend/plugins/mobilepress, if you would like to learn more).

You definitely want to be able to rank well, so you'll be glad to know the developer had SEO in mind. It will easily allow you to get indexed within the mobile searches from Google and other search engines.

Another neat feature is that you can create different mobile themes, if you'd prefer. There are other designers out there who have already done this. Themes can be determined on a device by device basis.

Mobilized by Mippin   this plug-in works a bit differently. This is a great plug-in for those have already signed up with Mippin and are looking for a way to redirect those mobile devices straight to your mobile Mippin site.

This plug-in is easy to use, and it's a no-brainer if you decided to go with Mippin.

Visit http://wordpress.org/extend/plugins/mobilize-by-mippin-wordpress-plugin/ for more information.

WordPress Mobile Edition this is a less commonly used plug-in, but it has great ratings as well. It, too, will render your site perfect for those on a mobile device. You can customize this, to a degree.

Visit http://wordpress.org/extend/plugins/wordpress-mobile-edition/ for more information and installation instructions.

WPtouch Pro this is not a free plug-in, but it just might be worth the cost for the serious business person. They call it "mobile streaming framework." It is easy to use. You can have the mobile version for your WordPress site set up in mere minutes. However, you can easily customize the theme or even build your own custom theme. It works with all of the most popular mobile devices.

Visit http://www.bravenewcode.com/products/wptouch-pro/ to learn more about the plug-in. This one comes highly recommended and people feel that it is worth the cost because it offers a seamless and professional experience.

Ensuring your mobile site is up to snuff.

You've definitely got to make sure your mobile site is everything you wanted to be in everything your users needed to be. One site you can use to do this is called MobiReady at http://mobiready.com. It's a free service, so there is no need to delay in ensuring your mobile site is up to standards today!

All you have to do is enter the URL of your mobile site. Then, you'll gain access to reports that let you know how well your site is performing. It will let you know if there are any potential issues, so you can quickly get on top of them.

View any site in mobile format this is a bit of a side note, but will likely be useful for you as you start to use your own mobile device more and more. Google has tools for everything else, why not a tool that automatically renders any website into a mobile website? Just go to Google mobile optimizer at http://www.google.com/gwt/n to take advantage of this, should you need to.

Mobile Payment Options as a marketer in a business person, the chances are very good that you like to make money from your mobile efforts. Good news! The mobile web can not only be used to expand your brand and share your content across different platforms, but you can also make some great money from it. The potential for this will only improve with time as more people a choir web compatible mobile devices and become more comfortable making payments through these devices.

There are many different ways to accept payments for mobile devices. You'll need to do a bit of research to choose the best option for you. There is no right solution for everyone! Some of these are fairly easy to implement while others are quite a bit more difficult.

Google Checkout Mobile Google is a well-known brand – – you can't escape it! That can be a good thing since your customers are likely to trust the Google name. It's even better if you're already using Google checkout on your website – – integration will be even smoother!

There is another **bonus** if you're a mobile ad words advertiser. *They will show your Google Check out badge right in the results! This can help improve conversion rates* since it stands out from other ads on the page.

What's really neat is that you don't have to do anything particularly special to display this mobile button on your site. It's the same code you would have on a standard website. It will show up in your customer's mobile browser window. When they click it, Google has a mobile version of their checkout page set up for them!

They've got some helpful information available for those wanting to make their sites more mobile friendly (beyond the suggestions I've already given you) found that: http://www.google.com/support/forum/p/checkout-merchants?hl=en.

Go to http://checkout.google.com/seller/mobile/index.html to sign up as a Google checkout seller and learned more about your mobile selling options with Google.

PayPal Mobile Checkout   If you're selling online, there is a high chance you're using PayPal. If you're not currently using them, you probably have in the past. Despite its quirks, it's an easy, and very popular, system for buyers and sellers. They offer mobile options too!

Here is how PayPal describes their mobile checkout process:

1. Your customers will click the "Checkout with PayPal" link or button on your mobile site or in an SMS text message.
2. They are taken to the PayPal site. They can login and choose the option they prefer.
3. The customer is sent back to your mobile site to complete the transaction.

To make things easy, PayPal allows customers to create a mobile pin for transactions.

It can be a bit complicated to integrate PayPal mobile property on your mobile site if you're not technologically inclined. PayPal has some feature cards you can use to make life easier.
Some of these include:

Billing Revolution at http://www.billingrevolution.com/

Mporia at http://mporia.com/

Cardinal Max at http://www.cardinalcommerce.com/max/

you can learn more about others, on our website for the rest of this article and more at: http://TheNewMarketingBasics.com/mobile. (coming soon, mobile that is.)

QR Codes

So, what is a QR Code?

They are barcodes on steroids, is the easiest way to explain them. You can tell a story, give contact information, give a phone number and have a one button call for the person reading the code. You can direct them to your website, collect their contact information, give them a coupon, and invite them to a party /sale / your business.

You can tell them about your upcoming sale. This handy dandy QR Code has the muscle to do so many functions that on our web site we have made available to you a FREE QR Code Generator.
www.thenewmarketingbasics.com/qr-code/qr-code-generator/

Go generate your own QR code for whatever you want to use it for and tell us about your uses and successes with this little square with code in it.

http://www.thenewmarketingbasics.com/qr-code/qr-code-generator/

 This QR code will take you to

www.theNewMarketingBasics.com QR Code Generator
Where you can make Your QR code and email it to yourself, FREE.

Come back any time and make as many as you like.
This is your private silent salesperson.

Disclaimer: we do collect your email address and we will send you at least 2 emails. The first one is a Thank You for choosing our Generator and the 2nd email is a follow up questionnaire, where we ask you questions about how you are using your QR code and what kind of response you are getting from your customers.

In that same questionnaire we will send you some Great tips from other people like you, who also will be sharing their ideas with us.

www.theNewMarketingBasics.com

10
TARGETING YOUR MARKETING EFFORTS

You might prefer one or the other but most likely your clients are made-up of businesses and homeowners.

While many of the marketing techniques you've already discovered in this report will help with both, there are a few tips you need to know that will help you market to each. And there are obvious differences between how you want to approach each one.

In general, when dealing with residential customers you want to remember to be warm. When dealing with commercial customers you can be a little less warm but more professional.

My experience in business has taught me that your image is critical to your success.

You will be inside your customer's homes, but before they let you in, you have to show them that you're not some Joe blow passing through town looking for beer money. Be Professional.

To that end it is critical that you utilize top quality marketing and business materials in order to ensure a 'good' first impression.

Private homeowners like to hire people they like and trust. They also want to like the person that's working for them. In fact, simply being well liked can ensure customer loyalty.

Here is a good place to remind you of an old adage #1

"The Customer signs your paycheck!"
This is very important to remember.

When talking to a Customer / potential Customer, Give Service, by being helpful, polite and fast to respond. Giving your Customers this type of service creates a cement type bond with your Customer.

Old adage #2, *"Customer is King"*, treat your Customers like that and they won't want to shop anywhere else. Would you?

However, with businesses, it's all about the business. They want a good job done.
If you don't do the work the way they want then they'll find someone else and they won't think twice about it.
Businesses want to be able to trust the people they hire to complete tasks for them and they usually don't want to be bothered beyond that.
Businesses will only be concerned with you providing great service.
Here you go the extra step and give them something that doesn't have much expense, but let's the Customer know that you appreciate them and their business.

Of all the residential customers the best prospects for your business are people who are wealthy. There are two reasons for this.
Number one they have the money to pay for what they want.
Number two they live in large homes and typically spend a large amount of money on home services and luxury items.

Let's take a look at targeting your marketing efforts to residential customers, commercial customers, and affluent customers.

Targeting Commercial Customers When you begin to target any specific type of customer, the first thing you always have to consider is what those customers want.
As we just discussed, businesses are mostly concerned with the job being done well. They also want to make sure you will get the job done when

it's supposed to be done without them worrying about it.
Other concerns for businesses, depending on the type of business, might be your appearance and the amount of money you charge.

You have to take each business individually and think about what they really want from a business.
The first two criteria – doing the job well and getting the job done on time – are givens but other criteria depend on the type of business and the people who run the business. For example, a restaurant would probably want a window cleaner that has a decent appearance and is able to be polite to their patrons.
But a small business that is isolated on a dead end street and makes yo-yos might not care how you look at all as long as you get the job done.

However, the yo-yo business might consider cost to be an issue.

For the most part you shouldn't ever play the money game. Your service is valuable and people will get what they pay for.
Ultimately it's up to you though.
But if you do offer your service at a discount for some businesses, you might find that those businesses require the most from you.

Now, the best way to attract commercial customers is through networking. You need to make some type of connection with businesses in your area.
Business owners are far more likely to hire you if they know who you are.
If your service is one that is used monthly then you might offer a 10% monthly discount if their payment is received before the 10th of the month that payment is due. Or cash on completion.
Not the 11th but before the 10th in your office.

I have used this one before and the customers that I offered the discount to ended up paying late and taking the discount. Not sure how to protect from this one but this is the reality of business. What I did was to not answer the customer when I was called back. This might not be the best thing to do either but it made me feel better. Best way is to carry the balance on the books and send out reminder invoices monthly that they failed to pay the proper amount. Be sure to add this amount on to any future billing.

The reason I have mentioned this here is that we want you to know what can happen. Reflecting back on this it would probably be best to offer a discount on future orders for the ones paid on time or early. This could put an end to the above practice.

Giving your customer this discount does a couple of things, gives your *good paying customers* a serious discount that they can really see and helps keep your money coming in on time.

A better way might be to offer the 12th month free if they pay the bill every month on time. This is less than 10% and seems like you're really giving value to your good customers. If you have a reoccurring service, window cleaning, office cleaning, pool service or really any monthly service.

Networking

One of the best ways to network is by joining your local chamber of commerce. Become active with it. Attend the meetings and any functions they might have.

You will meet many other business owners in your area.

With a decent elevator speech, you'll be able to attract customers this way.

You also want to attend any type of business functions that might be put on by other organizations. Get yourself out in public and make connections.

Chamber of Commerce, BBB, Toastmasters, Shriners, and more.

Being involved in charity events is another great way to network.

You will automatically be seen in a positive light by other business owners and you'll also have something in common with them from the start – being involved in charity work.

Networking is easily the best way to market to commercial customers.

Having a Website will help too.

So will word of mouth once you start getting some customers.

But to really make inroads with attracting commercial customers, you need to network. Just get to know the people behind the businesses in your area.

And let them know what you do and that you can really help them out with your service.

When you decide to target businesses make sure you call ahead and find out the name of the person who is in charge.

Also, find out the name of that person's assistant.

Then send postcards to each business that are addressed to the right person (make it personal).

Then follow-up with a phone call to the administrative assistant and inquire if they're interested in your service.

Often the administrative assistant helps make the day to day decisions like hiring people for a service, and the administrative assistant is much easier to get in touch with.

Targeting Residential Customers

Again, the first step to attracting residential customers is to think what they want.

They want someone who will do the job well, they want someone who is trustworthy, and they also want to know and like the person.

Let's break down those last 3 criteria because they're very important.

Homeowners first must trust you in order for them to hire you.

You can help them know you so it will be easier for them to Trust you.

This is always a key to someone making a purchase of any goods or services.

But with home services it's even more important.

Why is this?

Well, it's because you will see every room in their home, unless they pull the shades. But most windows don't have shades. So if you wanted to you could see an awful lot while providing a home service.

Homeowners also need to like the person who is providing a service for them.

They might not admit this last criteria but it's absolutely true.

Homeowners want to be able to know, like and trust the person who is working at their house.

Homeowners do not want someone they don't like coming to their home and performing a service.

In fact, people will overlook a couple minor mistakes if they like the person.

But most people won't be repeat customers for someone they don't like, no matter how well the job was done. Be polite.

So, the first step to attracting residential customers is to brand you as a nice and trustworthy company.

Remember that everything you do will be directly related to your business. So always portray the right image.

Right down to placing videos on your web site that introduce yourself and staff. This helps the Customer get to know how you work and what they can expect from you.

The more that you expand on this last idea, will expand your profits.

There are many techniques you can use to market to residential customers.

Many of these techniques have already been discussed.

But more traditional marketing techniques can be quite effective.

This includes sending out postcards about your business, sticking flyers up at all the local grocery stores (and community centers, etc.) dropping your business card off door to door, and sticking flyers under windshield wipers. Be careful here as a number of cities in California have made laws about putting fliers on car windows.

Going door to door and sticking flyers under windshield wipers is usually not very effective.

In fact, many people see this as more of an annoyance.

However, one way to do this type of marketing and have it be extremely successful is to give a free gift.

For example, you could order a thousand small bags and have something like "Here's a free bag of goodies, courtesy of (insert your business name here). Then you could put your contact information on the bag. Inside the bag you could have a gift that applies to the season.

This is a good idea to use in a strip mall where most of the businesses contribute something to the give-a-way that can be tied back to their business.
This method can be morphed to any number of marketing styles to suit anybody's style of marketing.

For example, if summer is coming up you could put a travel sized bottle of sun lotion, a bottle opener, and a magnet. Usually you can also have your business information printed on each free gift.

Giving free gifts will automatically make people like you. Everyone loves free stuff.
This is where coupon books work well (I have used these in a number of retail venues) and this gets the Customer to physically go to each business to redeem the coupons. (A 5% or 10% often times now is not enough to get people to buy, so make the offer worth 30% to 50% on one item. Just a suggestion.)

Marketing to Affluent Homeowners   Affluent people, people who have money and are looking to spend it for your service, are said to be completely different than people who don't have a lot of expendable income.
This is not completely true. However, it is true that you need to market to them differently.

Let's face it: The majority of your residential customers will be people who have money to spend. People who don't have any extra money can't afford to purchase home services or luxury items (at least not very often) and have houses that are small enough to do the house work themselves.

So you need to make sure you know how to market effectively to affluent customers.

To begin thinking about marketing to affluent people you have to think about what separates them from people who aren't affluent.
The answer, of course, is money. They have it. Others don't.

So money isn't much of a consideration for most of them. Usually affluent people will be willing to pay a large sum of money as long as the job is done the way they want it. And the way they want it might be very specific.

Now, the fact that rich people usually don't care too much about the cost of your service doesn't mean that you should jack-up your prices. It simply means that price should never be used as one of the selling points when marketing to them.

But let's take a closer look at what most affluent people want.
They want someone who is reliable and will do good work. In fact, often they have very specific instructions for how they want the job performed.
They also want to know that they have a real professional working on and around their home.

So you have to look and act the part. This means you need to be aware of your appearance and you also need to be aware of the appearance of the vehicle you drive.

Many affluent people love to impress their neighbors.
You may very well be part of their attempt to impress their neighbors.
This means you need to have a nice truck with your business name and logo on the door.

Keeping these things in mind, you'll be able to create the right marketing image.
But how do you actually get to market to these people?
Well, the methods aren't really any different than for other people.

One great form of publicity is simply being seen, working in the neighborhood.

People are much more likely to hire you if they see that you've done work for one of their neighbors.

With your truck parked out in front of the house, you'll be getting free publicity.

As with businesses, networking is a great way to market to affluent customers.

If you can get to know someone in an affluent neighborhood then you can open the door and you'll be able to attract more customers.

A few possible ways to help you network with affluent customers include: helping out with charities, joining a golf club or country club, and belonging to a neighborhood church.

Any association you can gain with people will help you tremendously.

But an association with people doesn't have to be through an organization. It can be through people too.

For this reason, make sure you give your elevator speech to your doctor the next time you visit him. Give your elevator speech to your accountant too. Give your elevator speech to anyone who is wealthy; in fact give it to everyone.

These affluent people might use your service, but more importantly, they might recommend your service to someone in their neighborhood.

It all comes down to opening up the market. If you have one customer from a neighborhood then many other neighbors are very likely to also take advantage of your business. Word of mouth is very powerful and so is having a presence in a specific area.

Summing-Up. Here we discussed targeting your marketing to specific groups of people. We looked at residential customers and commercial customers. We also looked at affluent customers.

You need to consider what people are looking for when they want a service done and then promise that. We went over this and we also looked at some marketing ideas for each group of people.

In the end it all comes down to creating a great brand and then getting the word out about your business.
Often the best publicity you can get is achieved through networking.
Make it easy for the Customer to find you on the Internet.
Have videos on your site to help your potential Customers get to know, like and trust you and your staff.

This will be time well spent and update your site(s) often.

www.theNewMarketingBasics.com

11

Polishing your marketing

Now we've reached the final chapter in this book and we're just about done. We're at the point in the report where we can sum everything up and add tips and tidbits that will make a good idea even better.

But before we build on everything that was already discussed in this report, we need to cover one more topic. That topic is press releases.

Press Releases

Press releases are the way you'll let the media know when you're doing something.
If you're offering something that's unique or something special has happened to your business then you can write a press release and send it to all the media in your area.

But you can't just decide to write a press release.
You have to have a reason.
You need to be announcing something that is newsworthy.
Here are a few examples of reasons you might write a press release:

Ø   Winning an award or being recognized in some other way.

Ø   Adding a new product line.

Ø   Sponsoring a charity event.

Ø   Team up with other businesses in the area

Ø   After a remodel of your business

Ø   Partnering with, merging with, or buying another business.

Ø   Gaining a contract with a large company.

Now, just because you write a press release and send it out doesn't mean that the media will pick it up.
If it's creative or timely then most likely it will get picked up.
This is where your use of marketing techniques will help get you and your business in front of the eyes, ears or both.

Press releases are awesome because they allow you to let get free publicity if one or more media outlets runs a story based on your press release.
A press release needs to be wrltten in a very specific way.

On Your Letterhead

Here is the format that should be followed: **(page 110)**

FOR IMMEDIATE RELEASE

Contact: (Your Name)

Phone Number: (Your Number)   925-555-1212

Cell Phone: (Your Cell)   xxx-xxx-xxxx

Email: (Your Email Address)

MAIN HEADLINE   (the Hook)

Subtitle of the Press Release

Main body (This is what you want to let people know. Use the upside down triangle just like newspaper articles do.)

###

For more information about the topic or to schedule an interview with (Insert Your Name), call at (Insert Number).

Where you see all capital letters used, make sure you use all capital letters.
Where it's centered on the page, make sure you center it, top to bottom and side to side.
Be sure to include three number symbols (### - this signifies the end of the copy) just like you see above and make sure you follow all the other formatting.

This is the way a press release is written.

As with everything else, the headline is very important and should include a hook.
Just remember you are sending this press release to the media.
They aren't interested in a cheap service or a special offer of any kind.

They are interested in things that will make a great story and things that others will find interesting, entertaining or compelling.
Make sure your hook is catered toward the media.

For the body of the press release you want to use what is called an upside down triangle? Sometimes it's also referred to as an inverted pyramid. This is the form you want to follow with all your press releases. It's also the way all newspaper articles are structured.

When you use an upside down triangle what you want to do is give all the broad and general information first.
Then you want to get more specific.
This way the reader gets all the important information first.
Then if and when they keep reading they'll be able to get the details.

Now you know the format for a press release but you don't know the exact information to put in it.
Remember that your goal isn't to blatantly market your business.
Your goal is to get picked up by news outlets.
For this reason steer clear of using all capital letters in the body of your press release and stay away from exclamation points. Also, don't write phrases like "call us today" or "discount prices" or "amazing deals."

Instead you want to include quotes from someone from the company (this will probably be you). Try to make the quotes seem like they came from an interview.
You should also include the, who, what, when, where and why.
If possible, throw some statistics in the press release too.

To get a general idea of what to write in a press release, read the newspaper and watch the news. Look for articles or stories about companies and see how they're written. This is how a press release should be written.

Once you have your press release all written, you can then email or fax it to all the local media.
You can compile your own list of email addresses and/or phone numbers

by calling each media outlet and asking them where you can send press releases.

You can hire a professional to write your press release for you. Some will distribute it for you too.
You can count on spending a decent chunk of money on this service.
But it's usually worth the cost, especially if you hate writing and aren't any good at it.

If you want a pro to write your press releases for you but you don't have a lot of money then you might be able to work out a discount that includes you doing some work for them in exchange for them writing your press releases. There are a number of places online where you can get something like this done on the cheap.

You can also write your own press release and use the Internet to distribute it.
4 of the top press release distribution sites are Marketwire (www.marketwire.com), PR Web Direct (www.prwebdirect.com), PR Newswire (www.prnewswire.com) and PR Leap (www.prleap.com).

It's all about the Customer

Obviously the success or failure of your business will come down to how many jobs you get or how much you sell. In other words, it will come down to what the customer spends.
But more specifically, it will come down to how many customers you can attract and how many customers you can turn into repeat and regular customers.

In fact, if most of the customers who hire you decide to keep hiring you then you'll be all set. And if those customers refer their friends and family to you then you'll be an overnight success story.

See why it's so important to make every customer happy?
If you really go above and beyond for your customer then that person is

likely to tell others how great you are and at least some of the people who hear how great you are will decide to hire you too.

Here are 3 tips for great customer service:

1. Always greet and treat the customer like they are absolutely the most important person in the world. They are the most important part of your business world right now. Don't ever forget that.

2. Always be able to answer questions in a knowledgeable way. Make sure you know everything you need to know so that you can be an expert in your field. What might seem like a harmless question from a customer may result in you losing their business if you're unable to answer that question.

3. Have a set process and policy for handling complaints. You might need to think about this one for a while.
But be consistent with the way you handle complaints, and make sure you always favor the customer.

The bottom line is this: It's much easier (and cheaper) to make money from existing customers then it is to get money from a potential customer.
Make sure that you do everything you can to retain as many customers as possible.

There are 2 great techniques for retaining customers.

The first is to have an active customer retention program.
This means you keep in contact with your customers.
You can do this with a newsletter, a postcard, or even a free gift.
Or all three.
Maybe send a small gift at Christmas (a calendar magnet with your logo on it is great) and a greeting card sometime in the spring.
Another very effective idea is to simply send a "Thank You" note after someone does business with you. Include a coupon for 25% off the next time they use your service. This will do wonders for your business. (The

amount of your discount is up to you.)
Just simple gestures like these will really help customers continue to do business with you.

The second great technique for retaining customers, deals with going after customers you might have lost.
Keep track of all your customers.
If it seems like you've lost a customer then send them a card and a discount coupon for their next purchase.

It's very simple to complete the first step of retaining customers. Treat them right and give them an incentive to continue to do business with you. Contact them often to keep you in front of them.
However, it's not so easy to keep track of and go after "lost" customers. But it's not rocket science either.

You can buy software that will keep track of customers and help you with customer retention. There are a few different software products. A couple of them can be found at http://www.maritz.com/tlps/Customer-Retention and
at http://www.managemore.com/crm/crm-learn.htm.
You can also use Microsoft Outlook which is a CRM of sorts.

However, unless you have a large business, you can probably set up your own customer retention program.
It can be as simple as putting all your customers into a basic spreadsheet. Plug in all their information and then color code them according to the time when they last purchased from you.
Usually the color coding is done for each year but it can be done at 6 month intervals or an even shorter amount of time.

For example, you might decide to highlight all your 2009 customers in blue.
Then in 2010 you'll highlight all your customers in yellow.
Then in 2011 you might go with pink.

Then you can look at your database of names and see which customers you've lost and when they were lost.

Another option would be to include a column for the year on the spreadsheet. Most spreadsheets allow you to search for numbers or words.
All you would need to do is update this column every time someone hires you and then just performs a search for a previous year and you'll find customers who've been lost.

The key is to keep your customers happy so they don't become lost customers.
But inevitably some people will drop off and these are the people you'll want to try to get back. You can call them or send them a postcard, or you could send them a survey.

Surveys are great because they make people feel like their opinion matters, they allow you to get in touch with lost customers, and they also allow you to find out the areas you need to improve. Don't send one every week unless it is part of your business plan.

Here is an example of a possible survey:

1. Our records indicate that you were a user of XYZ's service in the past but you haven't used XYZ service in over a year. Is this right?

O   Yes
O   No
O   I don't know.

2. What is the main reason you stopped using XYZ Company?

O   Cost
O   Treatment of Customer
O   Lack of Satisfaction with Service Provided
O   Other
O   I don't know.

Please explain other reason:_____

3.   Did you purchase XYZ service from another company?

O   Yes
O   No
O   I don't know.

4.   Is there anything that XYZ Company could do differently to keep your business? Please explain.

_____

From just those 4 questions you can find out a lot. And the survey is short enough to get a decent response.

With every reply you get you can not only try to get each individual customer back but you can also improve your overall business.

Remember, the best way to retain customers is to treat them well and provide a great service, with a fair price right from the start.

While you're at it, just as you did with lost customers, you might want to have current customers fill out a survey too.

You can offer a discount to customers in exchange for them filling out a short survey.

Then you can use their feedback for testimonials. You just have to get their permission to use their first name and you can do that by putting a little blurb on the survey that tells them the information they supply may be used for marketing purposes.

Referrals are Priceless

Finally, we already touched on how valuable word of mouth can be. Well you can help rocket that word of mouth by getting referrals from existing customers.

So many small business people who offer a service (just like you) fail to even think about referrals.

This is a huge mistake. Some marketing studies have shown that the average person is capable of making up to 50 referrals!

To run a successful referral program you just need to take care of three easy steps:

1. You need to do a great job for the customer.
2. You need to ask the customer to refer you.
3. You need to reward the customer for referring you to someone else. Here again offer a discount on future sale.

That's all there is to it. Just adopting this one change into your business will land you new customers almost immediately.

There are a lot of great referral programs out there.
One example is offering $50 to every person who refers a paying customer to you.
Or for 5 leads (5 names you can contact) you can give a customer 10 – 20 or 30% off their next purchase.

Again, depending on how large your business is, you might need software to help manage your referral program. But you can usually manage it yourself.
If you provide a great service and you treat your customers well then a referral program can be as easy as just creating a form that explains your referral program.
Then you can keep track of referrals on a basic spreadsheet.

It's Time to Use What You Discovered

So now you know a big part of this puzzle that you can use to effectively market your business.
The most important point you need to remember from this guide is that you must view everything as a marketing opportunity.
Absolutely everything!

And then you have to take advantage of each and every opportunity.
Take the time to make your USP / Elevator Pitch (that is your golden key)

and then build your marketing strategy around it.
Use as many of the great tips you just read about as you can.

Within just a few months, you'll see how much your business is helped
from your marketing efforts.
And as you test and modify your marketing plans, your business will only
get more successful.

Now, it's time for you to get started. It's time for you to truly market your
business and to finally achieve true success.

Marketing Materials Resource

With the above in mind I want to share with you one of my secret
weapons, that I use to ensure that all my marketing and promotion
materials are of top notch quality without breaking the bank.

The company is PsPrint and Vista Print, and they are in my opinion the
best professional online print shops around. They handle all my printing
needs for Postcards, Flyers, Door Hangers, Business Cards, Brochures and
Promotional Items. I even had them do a few Vinyl banners for me and
they turned out great!

Also if you need magnetic signs for your vehicle or yard/street signs for
your promotions, then I suggest you check out iPrint, as they have some
unbeatable pricing when it comes to these types of signs and even when
you add in shipping they are usually cheaper than your local sign shop.

www.theNewMarketingBasics.com
at the site you will also find:

Making money through mobile ads on your site.

How to get traffic to your mobile website

Redirecting regular site traffic

Paying for ads

Mobile SEO

And you'll find our list of mobile directories.

Off-line promotions

Add a bookmark button

We will be adding content often.

www.theNewMarketingBasics.com

Glossary

(most definitions from Wikipedia.org)

5 W's   Who is it about. What your specialty is. What you do to solve their problem.
Why you are better than the competition. What they need to do to take advantage of your business, be specific, say it. It needs to be a call to action, the close.

Auto Responder   Is a computer program that automatically answers e-mail sent to it. They can be very simple or quite complex and can be one of your best employee that works the hardest and gets paid the least.

Brand / branding A brand is the identity of a specific product, service, or business. A brand can take many forms, including a name, sign, symbol, logo, uniform, colors used in all aspects of your business. This can even include the way in which you answer the phone or email or???? By creating a strong brand in your product or business you give the consumer something to recognize there for they want to shop with you because of your strong brand.

Delicious Is a social Bookmarking service, which means you can save all your bookmarks online, shares them with other people, and see what other people are bookmarking. This also means that they can show you the most popular bookmarks being saved right now across many areas of interest. They also have search and tagging tools to help you keep track of your entire bookmark collection and find tasty new bookmarks from people like you. The biggest collection of bookmarks in the world.

Digg Online social news website made for people to discover and share content from anywhere on the internet, by submitting links & stories, and voting and commenting on submitted links and stories.

Elevator pitch or USP: an effective elevator pitch is designed to give the audience just enough information that they have a sense of what you are talking about and want to know more. Just as importantly, and an effective elevator pitch is designed to not give the audience so much information that they feel overwhelmed and tune you out. Your elevator pitch should be about 30 seconds long and no more than 2 min. We lean towards 30 seconds or less, which is about 90 words. Most won't listen for more than 15 seconds; if you're a fast talker then you'll rock.

Facebook Is a social networking website that allows you to share pictures, stories and friends, a place to share connections of friends and family, owned and operated by Facebook.

Keyword and indexing term, subject term, subject heading, or descriptor, is a term that captures the essence of a topic in a document. A way to organize and disseminate documents.

Keyword phrase a group of more than 2 words that makes up a search term.

Keyword tool software used to conduct keyword research showing the kind of searches being carried out by users and how often.

LinkedIn Is a business-oriented social networking site; it's mainly used for professional networking, or called business-to-business.

Link Wheel One great way to get a ton of traffic to your websites is to build a link wheel. These link wheels build back links to your websites main page, which gives your website higher search engine ranking.

Marketing plan   Is a written document that details the necessary actions to achieve one or more marketing objectives. This is where you will list your advertising strategy, and how you will use it to take advantage of the market place. Also see chapter Two.

Mashable an Internet news blog, with a reported 7+ million monthly page views self-reported and the Alexa ranking of just over 400, it ranks as one of the largest blogs on the Internet. It is also the top source for news in the social and digital media, technology and web culture. With more than 40 million monthly page views, Mashable is the most prolific new site reporting breaking Web news, providing analysis of trends, reviewing new websites and services, and offering social media resources and guides. Mashable's audience includes early adopters, social media enthusiast, entrepreneurs, influencers, brands and corporations, marketing, PR and advertising agencies, web 2.0 aficionados and technology journalist. Mashable is also popular with bloggers, twitter and Facebook users – an increasingly influential demographic.

Meta-tags The meta-description tag and the meta-keyword tag are not seen by the user. Instead these tags main purpose is providing meta-document data to the user agents, such as search engine.

Multiple keywords (phrase)   Groups of keywords or keyword phrases that make up your keyword lists for your product or service.

MySpace is also a social network site much like others that we've talked about. Always a good place to share stories pictures with friends.

QR Codes are bar codes on steroids. A square box that uses what looks like spots. Use these codes to communicate with your smart phone customers, by taking them to a web site or a sales video, tell them about upcoming events. Take them to a YouTube video, give them a coupon right to their phone to use now, inside (your store).

First use as the story goes by one of the major auto maker was using them for keeping track of unassembled car parts and have been morphed into a tool that all of us in business can use.

These code are read by a app that you can get for your cell phone and most of them are Free. My personal favorite is i-nigma from 3GVision at

http://www.i-nigma.com/Downloadi-nigmaReader.html.

Reddit where users (also referred to as Redditors) have the option to submit links to content on the Internet or submit "self" post that contain original, user submitted text. Other users may vote the post links "up" or "down" with the most successful links gaining prominence by reaching the front page. In addition, users can comment on posted links and reply to other commenters consequently forming an online community. Reddit users may create their own topical sections, known informally as sub Reddits and officially as communities, for which to submit their links and to comment, while appealing to a specific niche.

RELEVANCE of KEYWORDS: when you're searching your keywords be sure you keep this in mind that the relevance of keywords matter also. Not only exact word matches. (Relevance = Relating to the matter in hand) You would be surprised how well that works.

Social Marketing Is the systematic application of marketing through the use of social media sites. This can be stories of your use of the product, much like testimonial s. The difference is in social media you are personally telling your friends and family about your use of the product or service. This type of testimonial is better than one that comes from someone you don't know. That is why it is so powerful.

Split Testing When selling a product this is a way for learning a multitude of things about your product or service. For example: Which price will your product or service sell better at, to also give a better profit margin? Which display of your product or service does the customer prefer? What demographics does your product or service sell best to? ; This way you get information about your sales process as well. How the customer prefers to purchase your product or service, cash, credit card, check, or PayPal. This term can make you money just by finding the sweet spot.

StumbleUpon An internet community that allows its users to discover and rate Web Pages, photos, and videos. A new way to explore photos, videos, and web pages, recommended by friends and people sharing your interests. StumbleUpon learns what you like, so you only see what's interesting to you from across the web. Free to join.

It is a personalized recommendation engine which uses peer and social-networking principles.

Tags   in general tagging can be defined as the practice of creating and managing labels that categorize content using simple keywords.

Twitter   Is a social networking and micro blogging service that allows you to answer the question, "What are you doing?" by sending short text messages of 140 charters or less.

USP or elevator pitch: or more commonly known as Unique Selling Position or Proposition.
"U" is unique, what sets you apart from your competition and / or what is unique about your product or service?
"S" is selling, why the customer should buy from you?
"P" is position or proposition where you place yourself in a relationship to your competition, how / why you are a better choice.

Xomba is a community driven, instant publishing platform found on the principles of sharing revenue with its members. This is a playground for the budding writer in the serious freelance writer alike. Within their cyber walls will be found of virtual venue of soft pastels upon which to get your creative juices. This is quite possibly one of the best designed (or at least easy on the eyes) instant publishing platform on the Internet. It's a very attractive web property with simple to use and easy to read tab system of navigation. The design and presentation wasn't as smooth and easy as it is some might even call it functionality Spartan.

YouTube is a video sharing site on which users can upload and share videos. You can post your videos on YouTube and use its imbedded link on your site so that you are not hosting the video.

ABOUT THE AUTHORS

Thom has been in sales, marketing, and advertising for more than 45 years. He has trained as a professional salesperson. As a Teamster he ran a bread route in Silicon Valley for 30 years, where for 10 of those years his route was number one in sales.

Thomas created his own products (anti-siphon device) published booklets and been an Cross Bow Mail Order dealer. Sold lamps, Christmas Cards, Cowboy Hats and feathers as well as temporary Tattoos before they were the rage. All of those at the San Jose Flea Market.

He has created marketing methods that most laughed at but they worked.

Bill and Thom met in Las Vegas at a Practical Profits Seminar, started talking found out that we both lived in the same town and the rest is history. They have collaborated on a number of projects and you can expect more in the future.

Bill is the owner, publisher, and chief marketer at Internet–marketing–muscle.com, where he helps businesses and entrepreneurs get more customers and earn greater profits using proven Internet marketing techniques.

He also runs – with Thom 2 Meetup Groups in the East Bay area, one about capital SEO in Walnut Creek, California and the other about general Internet Marketing Tactics in Livermore California.

He offers a number of services, including – but not limited to – the following:

Website Development

Search Engine Optimization (SEO)

Google places page development

Facebook fanpage creation

Social Media Optimization (SMO)

in-depth Keyword Analysis

**FREE Membership for you at www.thenewmarketingbasics.com for 1 year when you purchase this book. from an authorized retailer. Just send a copy of your sales receipt to thom@thenewmarketingbasics.com and I will by hand (sorry but this part is not automatic yet) set up your FREE membership and email your password to you within 48 hours.

Please place the word "NMB membership" in the subject line for faster service.

Thank You and we hope that you enjoy this book and the web site.

Thom

&

Bill

www.ingramcontent.com/pod-product-compliance
Lightning Source LLC
Chambersburg PA
CBHW051536170526
45165CB00002B/751